WRESTLING
for BEGINNERS

WRESTLING
for BEGINNERS

TOM JARMAN AND REID HANLEY

CONTEMPORARY BOOKS

Library of Congress Cataloging-in-Publication Data

Jarman, Tom.
    Wrestling for beginners.

        Includes index.
        1. Wrestling.   I. Hanley, Reid M., 1945-.
    II. Title.
    GV1195.J38   1983   796.8'12   82-22042
    ISBN 0-8092-5656-8

Cover photos by John Morrison
Interior photos by Norm Cohen

Published by Contemporary Books
A division of NTC/Contemporary Publishing Group, Inc.
4255 West Touhy Avenue, Lincolnwood (Chicago), Illinois 60712-1975 U.S.A.
Copyright © 1983 by Tom Jarman and Reid Hanley
Printed in the United States of America
International Standard Book Number: 0-8092-5656-8
        05 06 QF 31 30 29 28 27 26 25 24 23 22 21 20 19

Contents

PART III: MOVES AND HOLDS

Foreword

In the past few decades wrestling has experienced dramatic growth, both in number of participants and in number of spectators. Refinement of the rules, intended to protect the participant and increase spectator interest, is one reason for the sport's burgeoning popularity. Improved equipment and coaching techniques have also furthered the sport. And televised Olympic wrestling matches and national collegiate championship competitions have shown the public once and for all that there is no similarity between amateur wrestling and the professional version.

Increasing numbers of parents, school officials, and, most important, athletes have come to recognize the great worth of amateur wrestling. It provides many unusual benefits. For example, individuals of any size and any age can compete, including those handicapped by hearing, sight, and limb defects. Wrestling also offers athletes the opportunity to enhance their self-confidence, strength, and endurance. Wrestlers not only learn athletic skills and techniques but also gain insight into their own character. And the sport can teach them lessons they will value for a lifetime—the art of self-discipline and sacrifice and how to exercise the will to prevail.

One of the great values of wrestling is learning to depend on yourself. You meet your opponent alone. Win, lose, or draw, you receive credit for your effort. Unlike team sports, there are no hidden or unsung heroes. The athlete can understand his true worth as he goes it alone.

Along with the benefits it offers, wrestling also makes certain demands on its athletes. The most basic of these probably is the patience and determination to establish a solid foundation in the sport. The beginning wrestler must take great care to learn the proper execution of basic holds. He should concentrate on a few holds and gradually develop the skills and maneuvers that fit his unique physical makeup. Novice wrestlers must strictly adhere to the fundamentals and must always remember that *fundamental* does not mean *simple*. The hard-earned mastery of fundamentals is vital for success.

Regardless of his level of competition, the successful wrestler must also reach the peak of physical conditioning. He must recognize the fact that his endurance cannot be built up until he has pushed himself past the point of being tired. This calls for great determination and courage—qualities that cannot be replaced by taking any easy way out or looking for shortcuts. There is simply little hope of defeating a man who is in better condition than you are.

Beginning wrestlers will find this book a valuable tool that will serve as their guide to a successful career. It contains the basics of a simple, yet complicated sport in readable form with many action photographs. For all levels of competition, the basics are essential to success. The techniques described and illustrated in this book will serve as the beginning point for wrestlers whose careers might extend into college competition and beyond. The fundamentals of the sport, along with its philosophies, strategies, and conditioning techniques, are detailed for the beginner and will serve as a reference source as he progresses.

Wrestling for Beginners will help establish a foundation for building a successful future in the sport and in life. It is a future that is attainable through dedication, sacrifice, and the will to achieve.

Paul K. Scott
Coach of Cornell College's 1947
NCAA and AAU champions
and member of the Iowa Wrestling Hall of Fame

Acknowledgments

Wrestling for Beginners isn't all Tom Jarman and Reid Hanley. This project would have never been completed if it had not been for the help and encouragement of friends and family.

Norm Cohen provided us with the photographs that complement the wrestling philosophy and style of Tom Jarman. Norm's patience and eagerness to please helped make the photo sessions successful. Tim Cysewski and Pete Galea, who are on the coaching staff at Northwestern, couldn't have been more cooperative in serving as models for the photographs. Young wrestlers who follow their examples will go far.

Jim Binkley and Karen Hanley provided help down the stretch that proved invaluable. Jim's editing skills gave the authors another point of view, and *Wrestling for Beginners* and its readers will profit from his help. Karen's typing skills and support went far beyond what can be expcted of even a spouse. The entire Jarman family is to be thanked for putting up with late night phone calls, messages, and meetings disrupting their lives for six months.

The United States Wrestling Federation was extremely helpful. Steve Combs and his staff provided photographs and valuable information that add greatly to this book.

Thank you all.

WRESTLING
for BEGINNERS

Part I: The Foundation

1

Introduction

Wrestling is one of man's oldest sports, but many people really don't know what it is.

It's not "sleeper holds," "airplane spins," or "pile drivers." Those terms describe the sort of action that you'll see in our sport's distant relative, professional wrestling. And professional wrestling is closer to entertainment than it is to sport.

Then what is wrestling?

- It's an increasingly popular sport that requires *strength, flexibility,* and *conditioning* of its athletes.
- It's an individual sport. A wrestler can't hide behind his teammates. He must accept the fame for winning and take the blame for losing. The wrestler can't blame the guy who blew the double play or missed a tackle.
- It's not a lonely sport. Sure, it's just you and your opponent out there on the mat, but even in an individual sport you need help. You'll need the cooperation and encouragement of your teammates, the enthusiasm and knowledge of your

3

There is no set age to start wrestling, but you're never too young.

coach, and the understanding and support of your friends and family.

- It is one of the fairest sports in that it favors no particular size or stature among wrestlers. Only in the heavyweight division is there any weight advantage. Athletes must meet a certain weight limit to compete. It is a sport for all sizes. There is room for everyone. Handicapped wrestlers, such as those who are blind or deaf, can compete successfully.

What is the object of wrestling? The ultimate object is to put your opponent's shoulders to the mat—to *pin* him. Pinning is not always possible when two well-conditioned athletes meet, so a scoring system has been developed to determine who has won. The basic concept of wrestling is simple. The wrestler tries to take his opponent to the mat; his opponent tries to get away from him

Wrestling isn't an easy sport, but the benefits are many. Winning is not the sole measure of the sport; doing your best is.

or reverse positions with him. The wrestler tries to turn his opponent to his back. The maneuvers used to accomplish these relatively simple goals are not so simple, and they number in the thousands.

THE BASICS OF A WRESTLING MATCH

When a wrestler takes his opponent to the mat and gains control of him, that's called a *takedown*, and it's worth two points. If the wrestler in the bottom position changes position and takes control on top, that's a *reversal*, and it's worth two points. If a wrestler gets away from his opponent, that's an *escape*, and it's worth one point. When a wrestler puts his opponent's shoulders within four inches of the mat, that's a *nearfall*, and it's worth two or three points, depending on how long he holds them near the mat.

There are three prominent styles of wrestling in this country.

The American style, used primarily in high school and college competition, is called *folkstyle*. *Freestyle* is the international cousin of folkstyle and is used in the Olympics. Folkstyle and freestyle are very similar. *Greco-Roman* is a form of wrestling used in the Olympics that permits neither the use of the legs in holds nor holds below the waist.

The first period, the length of which depends on the level of competition, begins with both wrestlers on their feet, which is the neutral position. Each wrestler will attempt to get a takedown in hopes of pinning the opponent. In a match, wrestler A takes down B and is ahead 2-0.

In the second period a coin is flipped to see which wrestler will be on top and which wrestler on the bottom. (These positions will be shown in a later chapter.) Wrestler A wins the flip and chooses to be on top. Wrestler B is down and will attempt to break free or change positions (reverse) with wrestler A. Wrestler B reverses his opponent and earns two points to tie the match at 2-2.

Wrestler A will start the third period in the down position since he was in the top position in the second period. If he breaks free, he gains a point for an escape and can go ahead 3-2. A breaks free to gain the lead but is then taken down by B for a 4-3 score. Wrestler A, however, comes back for a reversal to narrow the score to 6-5. Wrestler A then holds B's shoulders to the mat for a pin, which is also known as a fall, and the match is over.

COMPETITION FOR ALL AGES

There is no optimum age at which beginners should start wrestling prior to high school. Youngsters naturally tussle at a young age, and youth wrestling programs, sponsored by organizations such as the United States Wrestling Federation or the YMCA, take that impromptu play a step further. Basic holds and techniques, such as those shown in this book, are taught there. Various levels of competition, ranging from tournaments in which everyone gets a ribbon to national championships, are offered by the U.S. Wrestling Federation.

Junior high and high school competition are the next levels. Most U.S. high schools have wrestling programs, and many of them offer competition on junior varsity and varsity levels. Varsity competition consists of *dual meets* against one other school and *tournaments* involving several schools.

College competition includes schools of all sizes. College matches are longer since the athletes are older and stronger, but the sport is basically the same with some minor rule changes. National championships are conducted on all levels.

For wrestlers who are not in college as well as for college wrestlers during the off-season, there are *open competitions*. These tournaments might be between neighboring athletes or even between different countries. National and world open championships are conducted on several levels.

The top achievement in wrestling is the Olympic gold medal. Wrestling is one of the most competitive sports in the Olympic Games, and the United States has done well in recent Olympic competitions.

A WORD TO THE BEGINNER

To be a successful wrestler you'll have to work hard, watch your eating habits, and build your body. It isn't easy, so why do it?

Wrestling helps athletes develop in several areas. Briefly, it offers these benefits:

- You will develop physically in strength, stamina, and flexibility.
- You will also develop mentally through the use of different techniques and strategies.
- You will gain an understanding of the human body and how it works.
- You will develop socially as you learn to work with others, to interact with an opponent, to respond to an authority figure, and to follow rules.

- Wrestling helps you grow emotionally as you learn to deal with success and failure.
- Spiritual development comes in the form of courage and perseverance.
- It is also fun. Wrestling brings together people from all walks of life, all of them striving to be the best wrestlers they can be.

In short, if you've decided to become a wrestler, you've chosen to participate in the sport of philosophers and kings. In ancient Greece, the birthplace of Western culture, wrestling was considered an important element in one's education and development. The sport had educational, social, and religious significance in that culture, and it still offers such benefits to participants. To elaborate, young wrestlers can look forward to the following rewards.

Wrestling certainly can contribute to your personal development. Physically it will improve your strength, flexibility, and *endurance*, as well as your *balance* and *coordination* skills. Mentally, concentration, the learning of technique and strategy, and problem solving are all part of this sport. Socially, wrestling demands that team members work cooperatively toward a common goal. Wrestlers tend to be empathetic toward those around them. They must learn to function within a rule system and with various authority figures. There is ample opportunity to develop leadership qualities. Emotionally, the young wrestler learns to deal with success and failure, good breaks and bad breaks. Wrestlers develop the ability to function as individuals along with the capacity to cope with the accompanying stress of wrestling competition.

Wrestlers tend to develop great spirit. Their perseverance and courage are tested daily, not just in competition. When competition does take place, however, it can reveal a lot about the athletes' character.

Overemphasizing winning or even performing can ruin your athletic experience. Let the coach—not your friends, your parents, or yourself—handle evaluations, especially negative ap-

Wrestling is an individual sport, but the whole family can participate in it and even enjoy it from the sidelines.

praisals of your performance. Be sure to keep the educational objectives of the wrestling experience in mind or you will risk losing all perspective on the athletic experience.

Wrestling is a great sport, but athletes must remember that it is still just a game. Too often in our sports culture the successful athlete becomes a prima donna. So it is important that your athletic demands do not throw your family into disarray. Wrestling should enhance family life, not dominate it. Family members should offer support to you as you carry the family colors into competition. In turn, you should support the efforts they make in your behalf. Competitions provide opportunities for family outings and travel and bring the family together in a common purpose. Wrestling should be great fun for all of you.

You and your family must realize that wrestling is a very difficult sport. It is anaerobic in nature, which means that the wrestler's physiological system cannot sustain continuous exercise, so fatigue is great. You may spend as many calories in one practice as a normal adult spends in four days. Special attention must be paid to your nutritional and sleep habits.

Wrestling is a safe sport, and serious injuries rarely occur. There are however, constant bumps, bruises, and strains because of the contact nature of the sport. You will find that these nagging injuries contribute to your toughness. You will soon learn that you are capable of functioning well despite a few minor aches and pains. You may even be slightly proud of these temporary combat scars. Nevertheless, make sure your home medicine cabinet contains plenty of antiseptic and your freezer stocks lots of ice.

You'll probably find that your parents are proud of and enthusiastic about your wrestling. They will watch you take the mat alone and mature before their very eyes. They will cry and laugh with you, and your family will grow closer through it all. Welcome to the adventure of wrestling!

HISTORY

Organized wrestling for boys began only about 20 years ago, but wrestling isn't a fad. It is as old as civilization itself.

The earliest accounts of wrestling date back to Mesopotamia some 5,000 years ago. And even in its early stages, the sport was sophisticated. Monuments, art works, and hieroglyphics attest to the highly developed techniques used by early wrestlers, and the tomb of Beni Hasan in Egypt, which has been dated at 2000 B.C., shows a wide variety of wrestling holds. Most of our present-day holds were invented during wrestling's early days.

The center of wrestling moved away from Egypt and Assyria as the power of the world shifted to Greece. Athenian hero Theseus introduced the sport to the Greeks. Theseus proved that *technique* could overcome strength when he defeated strongman Broyon in a match. This event helped the sport develop into an art and a science. Wrestling became more than just a sport. It was a part of the Greek way of life. The poet Homer chronicles some of the Greek bouts, the most famous being between Ajax and Odysseus. Wrestling enjoyed the popularity that golf and bowling do today in our society, and it was not uncommon to invite a friend over to wrestle.

Wrestling was also included in early Olympic Games. It was first introduced into the games in the 18th Olympiad in 704 B.C. Greek Poet Pindar claimed that the Olympic Games came into being in 776 B.C. as a result of a wrestling match between the gods Zeus and Cronus.

Wrestling is also mentioned several times in the Bible. The most prominent Biblical reference is that of Jacob wrestling with the angel of the Lord one night.

The Roman Empire embraced wrestling with the same fervor as the Greeks had, and the Romans developed what we now call the Greco-Roman style. They adapted the sport to their own traditions and refined it, barring some of wrestling's cruel features. With the fall of the Roman Empire, wrestling lost some of its popularity.

Europe came to enjoy the sport, and one of the most famous matches was between Henry VIII of England and Francis I of France. There are conflicting versions of what happened when the two monarchs wrestled. In one version Henry challenged Francis to a match. In another Francis became angry when Henry made fun of the French wrestlers during a competition between the two countries, and Francis challenged Henry. Francis used his technique and cunning to overcome Henry's strength and pinned him.

The Asians developed their own style of wrestling. Japanese sumo wrestling is still practiced today, with one big difference—matches are no longer fought to the death.

Wrestling arrived in North America long before the Pilgrims. The Indians were the first wrestlers on the continent.

According to the U.S. Wrestling Federation, seven United States presidents were wrestlers, including George Washington, whose skill as a wrestler in the "collar and elbow" style preceded his fame as a general and the father of our country. But Abraham Lincoln's prowess probably made him the best-known wrestling president. Lincoln had strength that belied his lanky frame and was highly proficient in "catch-as-catch-can" style. His match with a local roughneck, Jack Armstrong, gave him the reputation of being nearly unbeatable. Lincoln did meet his match in Lorenzo D. Thompson. Thompson threw him the first time, and in the second fall both wrestlers went down. Lincoln, true to the nickname Honest Abe, did not call the match a draw.

Zachary Taylor, U. S. Grant, Andrew Jackson, William Howard Taft, and Theodore Roosevelt were other U.S. presidents with wrestling backgrounds.

In its early days professional wrestling was not farcical, as it is today. Frank Gotch of Humboldt, Iowa, has been acclaimed as the greatest professional wrestler of all time. When he died in 1917 the real sport of professional wrestling died with him.

The formation of the Amateur Athletic Union in 1888 divided wrestling into professional and amateur competition. Weight classes were established, laying the foundation for the fairest of all sports, today's wrestling. The first college dual meet was between Yale and Columbia in 1903, and the first *National Collegiate Athletic Association* championships were held in 1928 at Iowa State University in Ames.

Wrestling is now the fifth-largest sport in the United States on the high school level, with nearly a million participants. The U.S. Wrestling Federation has kids' programs in 35 states and conducts numerous competitions, including the *U.S. Kids Championships* and the *USWF* National Junior Championships.

The sport is no longer just a winter activity. Competitions are held in freestyle and Greco-Roman styles when school seasons are over. And college wrestling is no longer the end of the competitive line, with wrestling clubs becoming more prevalent. The United States has made great strides recently on the international level with the U.S. Wrestling team winning six medals in the 1976 Olympics, and the opportunities for wrestlers have never been greater.

2

Conditioning

As a serious athlete, you must build your strength and stay in condition to meet the challenge of wrestling. Wrestling isn't an easy sport, and the physical demands on you will be great. The rewards in general health and personal satisfaction are also great and can be obtained through sound conditioning.

Condition is just one of the factors that can help make you successful as a wrestler. Although it is just one of the pieces necessary to build a good wrestling career, it is also one of the most important. It is the foundation. Without conditioning, natural athletic ability and wrestling technique are wasted. Conditioning alone won't consistently win matches, but, combined with technique and ability, it can provide the winning edge.

There are three basic components of conditioning: *exercise, nutrition,* and *rest.* Each area is equally important and shouldn't be overlooked. If one area is neglected, it limits the positive effects of the other two. For example, hard work such as running or weight training can be canceled out by a poor diet. And a good diet and exercise program will suffer if you don't get proper rest.

Being in top
condition has many
rewards, and winning
is just one of them.

EXERCISE

Exercise is the most obvious aspect of conditioning. The muscles of the body must be built up and kept in top condition. A basic program of different types of physical activities is needed to build flexibility, endurance, strength, coordination, and balance skills.

Building Endurance

Whether matches are three minutes, six minutes, or seven minutes long, endurance is the key. *Distance running* is one of the most neglected forms of conditioning. It will improve lung capacity and circulation. Not everyone enjoys running, but the benefits make the effort more than worth it. During the final minutes of a match any defeat can be turned into a victory if the endurance factor is in the wrestler's favor. As long as a wrestler has endurance and time on the clock, the match isn't over.

Running short distances also builds endurance. This doesn't mean running the length of the football field and then resting. That won't do. In the case of running short distances *(sprinting)*, repetitions are what count.

In running, start out training slowly and build up mileage and the number of sprints you do. Don't start running two miles and 15 sprints of 50 yards unless you are in condition to do so. Increase the distance as your endurance builds.

Increasing Strength

If everything else is equal, strength will always win. Without sufficient strength, you won't even be able to properly use the techniques.

Weight training is most crucial in building strength. A series of lifts, building different areas of the body, should be used. No areas of the body should be neglected. Big biceps can't make up for weak legs.

Weights aren't the only answer, however. Strength should also be built through a series of *calisthenics*. Push-ups develop arm and chest muscles, sit-ups work stomach muscles and build leg muscles, and bridging is very important in developing neck muscles. Rope climbing and pull-ups are, perhaps, most important.

Improving Coordination, Flexibility, and Balance

Not everyone is blessed with natural coordination, but that doesn't mean you can't become a well-coordinated wrestler through hard work. Jumping rope is a key exercise in developing coordination and in enhancing footwork and timing. It is also excellent for endurance. *Scrimmaging* aids coordination by allowing you to repeat actions used in an actual match. In wrestling, there is a need to be flexible, and continued practice in the sport will promote flexibility and balance skills.

NUTRITION

A balanced diet is another key factor in conditioning. All food groups, especially green vegetables, which have high nutritional values, are important to the development of the young athlete. Vitamins and minerals should supplement the diet, especially during weight cutting periods. Large amounts of water should also be consumed to replace the fluids lost during your athletic activities.

Young wrestlers burn energy at a high rate. To perform properly the body must be fueled with the right foods. Again, the wrong diet can harm your efforts in other areas. Strength and endurance can be reduced if the body does not get proper nourishment.

Meals should be eaten at regular hours. That doesn't mean that you can't make an occasional exception in your schedule or that dinner has to be eaten at exactly 6 p.m. It does mean a regular schedule of meals should be kept. Snacks, especially junk food, should be avoided. They might taste great at the time, but you will pay for them later.

It can never be stated strongly enough that athletes should avoid drugs, alcohol, and tobacco. Each one of them will rob your body of strength and willpower. These substances can also be habit forming and can only hinder your activities.

Weight control has been the downfall of many good wrestlers. Improper weight control, such as cutting down on eating too many meals or dieting too quickly, will sap your strength and diminish your skills. The wrestler must eat the proper foods, including fruits, vegetables, and whole grains and have the willpower to avoid junk foods that are harmful.

Diet is the key to weight control. Wrestlers compete in *weight classes* and must weigh in before matches. Finding the best weight class is a problem for the young athlete.

Most wrestlers want to compete in as low a weight class as

possible to gain a strength and size advantage, but weight cutting is seldom advisable for the growing athlete. Excessive fat should be lost, obviously, and dropping a couple of pounds should not be harmful, even at *optimal weight*.

A good rule to follow is to shed excess weight and then *stabilize* at that weight, if possible. If stabilization is not possible with a balanced diet, then move up a weight class and stabilize at that weight. Maintaining a reasonable weight is important and it can be done without diet aids through hard work and a balanced diet.

In determining the best weight, a wrestler may need the help of his parents, the family doctor, the coach, or a physical fitness professional. At health clubs, fitness centers, or sports medicine facilities, it is possible to get an estimate of your percentage of body fat. This is determined through the use of skin fold tests and body composition tests. Even with these sophisticated methods, there is no ideal percentage of fat an athlete should carry. Each person is different in build and body makeup.

Dehydration (loss of body fluids) occurs naturally during the course of a hard workout. Even if an attempt is made to replace liquids during practice, you will lose fluid through perspiration. This is called *acute dehydration*, and three to four pounds can be lost during one workout. The mature, trained athlete will lose up to 10 percent of his body weight through acute dehydration without any adverse effect on his performance. Dehydrating or drying out over several days is called *chronic dehydration* and should definitely be avoided.

If care is taken, you should have few problems in determining your best weight. Sometimes, however, a growing wrestler will struggle to maintain weight. Extremes in behavior, such as lethargy, hyperactivity, and crankiness, should be regarded as danger signs and the wrestler should move up a weight class. Extremes in the length of sleep periods or difficulty in falling asleep, listlessness or increased activity, anxiousness or apathy are all warning signals that the wrestler is not at his best weight. When there is doubt, move up a weight class. The increase in energy and positive attitude you receive will more than compensate for any size disadvantage.

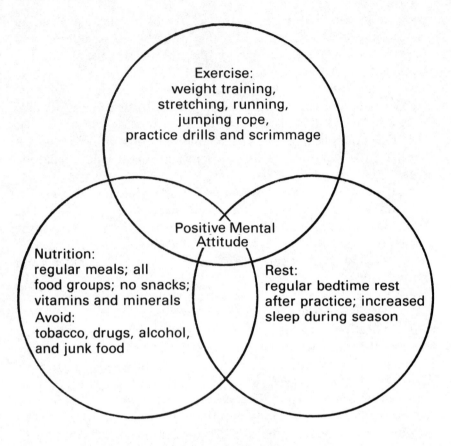

CONDITIONING

REST

All the strength, natural ability, and technique in the world won't suffice if your body is tired. The young body, in particular, needs rest. The demands of wrestling are so rigorous that the body needs time to recuperate to compensate for all the hard work it has done. Rest is the answer here.

Naps aren't just for babies. After a hard practice, a short rest period is helpful. A short nap is more beneficial than just lying around the house, because sleep will allow your body to recover from a good, hard workout in less time than just relaxing.

There is no set time when you should go to bed as long as you get a good night's sleep. Something can be said for going to bed early and getting up early, especially if morning activities are involved, for this gets your body going in a routine. Regardless of when you go to bed, however, get about eight hours of sleep per night. A regular bedtime and a consistent amount of sleep each night are preferred.

MENTAL CONDITIONING

Conditioning doesn't end with the body. The mind is just as important and can influence all other aspects of conditioning. Wrestlers must have a positive attitude. Physical conditioning isn't easy and often isn't fun. But it is worth it, and keeping the rewards for your efforts in mind will help you maintain a good attitude. To gain the winning edge over an opponent, you must carry out your training with dedication and optimism.

Athletes must discipline themselves to eat the right foods, do the right exercises, and get the right amount of rest. As a young wrestler, you must take charge of your conditioning. If you do, you will have the confidence in competition to win the big match.

An old saying might be helpful here: "To be a champion you have to practice like a champion." All exercise should be done to the maximum. Doing 50 push-ups, 48 of them perfect and two of them sloppy, counteracts the self-discipline that wrestling requires.

3

Strategy

Certain strategies, general principles, and attitudes have emerged in wrestling through the years. If you are to become a successful wrestler, you must develop proficiency in the following areas.

Aggressiveness. No other ingredient may be more apparent in champion wrestlers than aggressiveness. Even if you're not particularly assertive in other ways, you must be aggressive on the mat. You must take the match to your opponent. *Counter wrestlers*, who wait for the opponent to make the first move, invariably run into trouble as the competition gets tougher.

Match control. Aggressiveness may be the key factor in what is called match control. Match control is the match within the match. As the bout develops, each wrestler attempts to make his opponent react instead of act. The principle involved is that the acting wrestler will more often score points than the reacting opponent. Don't assume that this means you should try to get the upper hand with reckless abandon; remember the word *control*. To control the match you simply put as much pressure on the

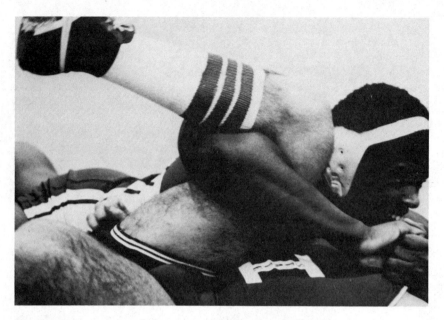

Pinning is the name of the game. Pinning is winning.

opponent as possible to keep him reacting throughout the match.

Situation wrestling. Situation wrestling is related to match control. The opponent reacts to the aggressor's attack with movements or counters. Knowing how to *key* off these counters, to finish a move or switch to other moves, is called situation wrestling.

Chain wrestling. Some wrestlers seem to *flow* through their moves. They have learned to chain wrestle. That means they automatically go from their takedown to a breakdown to a pinning combination. Chain wrestling also describes the flow of a wrestler moving smoothly from move to move in an attempt to escape or reverse his opponent.

Setups. To start a chain or series of moves effectively you must set up the initial move. In other words, an opening must be created for the attack. This is done in five basic ways: (1) by moving the opponent or part of his body into or away from the attack, whichever is desirable; (2) by changing level; (3) by motion, moving circularly inward or outward; (4) by making another move (one move tends to create opportunities for another move); (5) by faking a move or setup.

Finishes. A new wrestler soon finds that the move he starts is not necessarily the move he finally makes. Each move has several possible finishes. For example, a *double-leg attack* may end with a *trip,* a *lift,* a switch to a *single-leg attack,* or a drive across to the mat.

Upper body moves. As our style of wrestling is influenced by the international styles, we see more upper body moves. Some of these are illustrated in Part III in the section on takedowns. Upper body throws not only add more moves to a wrestler's style; they also help his strategy, because he can mix those throws with his leg attacks. For example, the wrestler can move from a double-leg attack into a *body lock* and *throw.*

Pinning. It is important to learn pinning holds right from the start. At first, young wrestlers are often encouraged to concentrate only on takedowns and escaping. This is poor advice for several reasons: (1) Scoring a fall is the ultimate objective in wrestling. No matter what the score, either wrestler can end the bout with a pin. (2) It is difficult to pick up pinning later in your career because most of the openings for a *pinning combination* occur during or immediately after a takedown or reversal. Pinning combinations must be developed early or they will not become part of the wrestler's working objective. (3) Putting an opponent on his back for a nearfall may be the easiest way to score in wrestling because most beginning wrestlers are not skilled at countering pin holds.

Mat savvy. Even the youngest of wrestlers must quickly develop what is called mat savvy. This involves keeping track of the score, listening to the coach, knowing how much time is left in the bout, knowing where you are on the mat and what the rules are concerning edge or out-of-bounds calls, sensing when to change the *pace* of a match, and *reading* an opponent.

Sportsmanship. The hothead, sulker, and show-off always have trouble in wrestling. Losing your temper or getting too emotional gives an easy advantage to a calculating opponent. Grumbling about officials' calls also breaks concentration, and no one appreciates a "hot dog" for very long. The poor sport relinquishes the objectivity of the referee, the respect of his opponent, the support of the fans, and ultimately a lot more. Wrestlers tend to be great competitors and good sportsmen. You should do your best to uphold this tradition.

Part II: The Seven Basic Skills

In the past, wrestling terminology and style varied widely from region to region. As a result, as many as four different names were often used for the same move. To standardize basic instruction and terminology, the U.S. Wrestling Federation's national coaching staff has divided wrestling skills into seven basic categories: *posture, motion, changing level, penetration, lifting, back-stepping,* and *back-arching.* These skills don't cover every possible action a wrestler may take, but they do provide a basic framework for learning technique. Chapters 4–10 will introduce you to the seven basic skills.

LEARNING FROM PICTURES

The pictures in this book are detailed studies. The two subjects in the photographs, former University of Iowa All-American Tim Cysewski and former Iowa State All-American Pete Galea, have both won national tournaments and were chosen because of their reputations for technique.

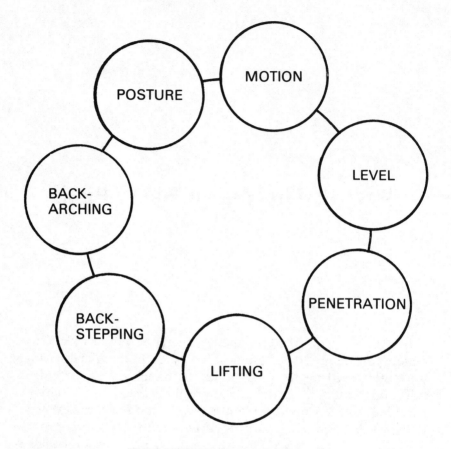

THE SEVEN BASIC SKILLS

Carefully study the subjects in each photograph. They represent ideal positions. A beginner might not be able to reproduce them perfectly, but this is not a cause for concern. Practice makes perfect.

Here are several suggestions for learning from pictures:

- Look through the entire sequence to get an overall idea of the maneuver.
- Focus on the wrestler in the black uniform, designated *B* in

the text, unless a counter move is being described. In that case, focus on *W*.

- Identify the key points of the description in the photos.
- Make your own observations about the photographs.
- Pay attention to the position and level of the offensive and defensive wrestlers. Can you determine why the move is effective?
- Try to copy the maneuvers pictured. This will aid in the learning process.

In Parts II and III photographs and text are closely coordinated. Refer back and forth from the pictures to the text until you understand each maneuver. Missing a key description or photo can lead to frustration when you attempt the move.

When you understand the maneuver fully, set aside the book and mentally picture the move step by step. Reading these parts of the book with a friend or drilling partner can be extremely helpful. After reading the descriptions and studying the photographs, immediately practice the moves to reinforce what you have learned.

4

Posture

Posture deals with the correct body position, not only in the various *starting positions* but also while going through the actual moves and counterattacks. More matches are won or lost because of body position than any other aspect of technique.

Wrestling posture begins with a good *stance*. In both the *neutral* and *referee's position*, it is important to keep the head up, the arms close to the body, and the feet, hips, and shoulders in good vertical position. Any time this *alignment* breaks down, your posture is poor. You are then vulnerable to attack and can be turned.

Figures 1–18 illustrate posture. Figures 1 and 2 show the proper neutral stance, which provides good stability as well as a base for movement. This is called an *even stance* because the feet are positioned so that neither one is ahead of the other. A *staggered stance* is pictured in Figures 3 and 4. You should be able to work from both stances.

Care must be taken to maintain good posture when in a *closed* or *tie-up* position. Proper position is maintained by the wrestlers

Figure 1

Figure 2

Figure 3

Figure 4

Figure 5

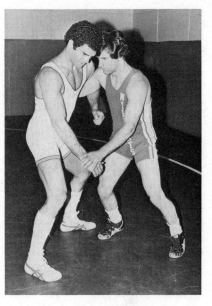

Figure 6

in Figure 5 (the head tie) and Figure 6 (the underhook tie).

Figures 7–9 show some common errors in posture. In Figure 7 the arms are not close to the body, allowing an opponent to attack underneath them. In Figure 8 the feet are spread too far apart, limiting the wrestler's ability to move forward or backward. In Figure 9 the head and back are held too low, making the wrestler vulnerable to a head attack or making it easy for him to be *snapped down* to the mat.

Figures 10–18 deal with posture position in the referee's position, which is the starting position of the wrestler on the mat before the whistle blows. The proper bottom stance is shown in Figures 10–12. Figure 10 shows the feet cocked; Figure 11 shows the feet hidden. Some wrestlers cock their feet for more power, while others hide their feet for protection against *ankle rides.*

The correct position is lost in Figure 13 because the wrestler is too far forward. In Figure 14 the head is too high and the back too flat, making it difficult for the wrestler to come off the whistle with power.

Figure 7   Figure 8

Figure 9

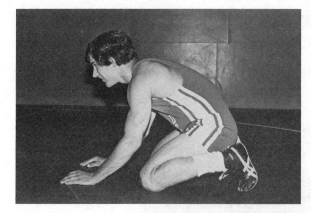

Figure 10

Figure 11

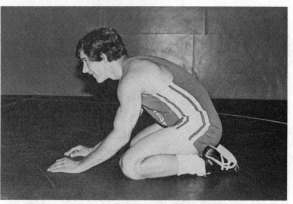

Figure 12

Figure 13

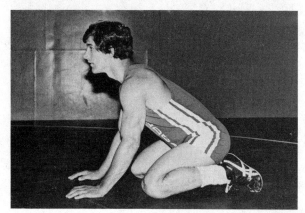

Figure 14

Figure 15

Figure 16

The top position is not too different from the bottom position. As shown in Figures 15 and 16, one knee is off the mat and one hand is placed around the opponent's waist and over his navel, while the other hand grasps his elbow. The key is good alignment over a base of support that allows movement in any direction.

The top wrestler in Figure 17 is too far back and is therefore limited in his ability to move. In Figure 18 he is too far forward and is vulnerable to *rolls*.

POINTS TO REMEMBER

- Good wrestling position allows you to defend and attack in all directions.
- To execute a good move, start from the proper stance and maintain good position throughout the maneuver.
- Constantly evaluate your position and stance.
- Stay in alignment, with your shoulders over your hips and your hips over your heels.
- When good position is lost it is usually best to bring your head up and curl the hips forward until alignment is restored.
- Good position can compensate for a weakness in balance by stabilizing you.

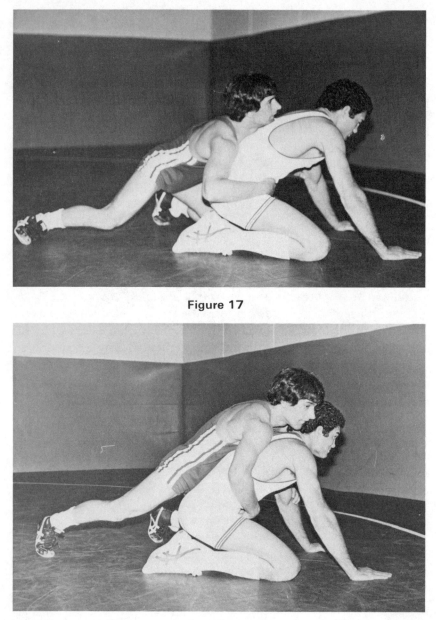

Figure 17

Figure 18

5

Motion

The ability to move properly is very important in wrestling. Speed is a wonderful gift for the wrestler to possess, but maintaining good position during movement is more important. Motion is used to defend, attack, and set up moves as well as to execute the maneuvers themselves.

Motion should never take you out of a good *base of support* or throw you off balance in any way. Young wrestlers will have to work hard to control motion. You must learn to move forward, backward, and sideways. These three types of motion are illustrated in Figures 19–27.

Your base of support is very important, especially in defending. When you attack, you can't give up that base. In most cases the foot closest to the direction of movement is the first to move. This widens your base of support. When the second foot moves, the original base is restored. You should attempt to keep your feet apart most of the time and should never cross your legs or feet.

Forward motion is pictured in Figures 19–21. Figure 19 shows

Figure 19

Figure 20

Figure 21

Figure 22

Figure 23   **Figure 24**

the wrestler beginning to lean forward in his stance for attack. In Figure 20 he has moved his *lead foot* forward, thus widening his base. He has brought the back foot up in Figure 21 to regain his original stance. If the wrestler moves his back foot first, he may move more quickly, but his feet will be dangerously close together and vulnerable to attack.

Backward motion occurs in the opposite fashion. Figure 22 shows the beginning stance. To move backward, the wrestler in Figure 23 has moved his back foot farther back. In Figure 24 the forward foot is drawn back into a normal stance.

You start lateral or circular motion moving the outside foot first and then the other foot. As shown in Figures 25–27, this widens the base and then closes it again to restore a good stance. In all the motion pictured the wrestler maintains good alignment of his body, hips, and head. His motion does not take him out of good posture.

Figure 25

Figure 26

Figure 27

POINTS TO REMEMBER

- Motion is used to attack, defend, set up, and execute moves.
- Motion should never take you out of good position.
- Motion should not throw you off balance.
- The foot closest to the direction of motion is the one to move first.
- The wrestler must work for hours and hours to perfect his motion.

6

Changing Levels

Changing levels involves the raising and lowering of your hips to set up, execute, finish, and counter moves. For some wrestlers this skill is difficult to perfect. It isn't actually changing levels that presents the problem, but maintenance of good posture as one does so. Strength and flexibility must be developed in the legs and hips, and good alignment must be maintained, if the level is to be changed effectively.

In setting up moves, level is lowered or raised to get past an opponent's defenses. Moves also can be set up by changing levels because a change forces the opponent to react by matching that level.

Figures 28–30 show how changes in level can be used against an opponent. In Figure 28 the two wrestlers are at approximately the same level. In order to create an opening, B raises his level as shown in Figure 29. Notice that W has matched B's level. In Figure 30, B has lowered his level and penetrated, taking advantage of the opening. Levels may change several times during the execution of a move to gain an advantage. Level changes are almost always involved in finishing moves.

Figure 28

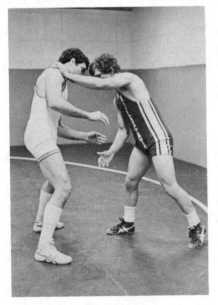

Figure 29

Figure 30

Figure 31

Figure 32

Figure 33

Figure 34

Figure 35

Figures 31–35 show level changes during execution of the double-leg attack. In Figure 31 wrestler B has moved into a closed position. In Figure 32 he lowers his level below the defenses of his opponent (W). He continues to lower during penetration (Figure 33) and then raises his level to finish penetration (Figure 34) and gain an *angle* on the opponent. Figure 35 shows what happened when he lowered the level again to finish the move.

The level changes are also critical in executing the high single-leg attack shown in Figures 36–39. In Figure 36, B lowers his level to attack W's leg. He raises his level again as he moves laterally in Figures 37 and 38. In Figure 39 he steps back, squats, and lowers his level to snap W to the mat.

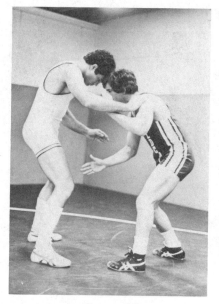

Figure 36

Figure 37

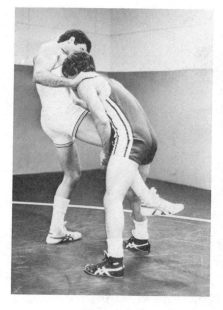

Figure 38

Figure 39

Figure 40   Figure 41

Figure 42

Level changes are important in the *center step single-leg attack*, which finishes with a lift, illustrated in Figures 40–45. Level is lowered during the setup and penetration and then raised to complete the lift, only to be lowered again to finish.

Figure 43

Figure 44

Figure 45

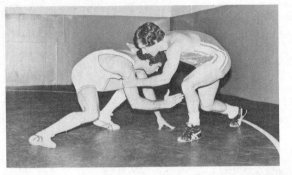

Figure **46**

Figure **47**

Figure **48**

Level is often lowered to counter an attack. In Figure 46, B lowers his level as W starts his penetration. In Figure 47, B has further lowered his level, sprawled his legs back, and started to *crossface* and spin to counter. B has turned the corner in Figure 48 and destroyed W's alignment.

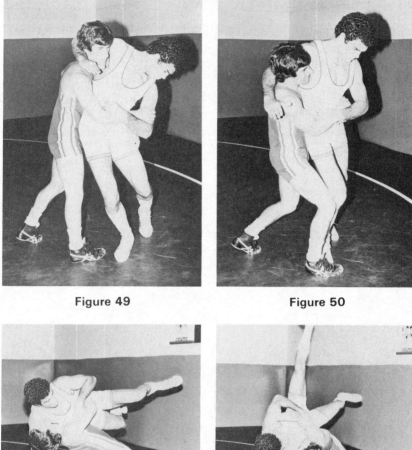

Figure 49   Figure 50

Figure 51   Figure 52

Changing level to counter a *headlock* is seen in Figures 49–52. In Figure 49, W has attempted a headlock. To counter, B lowers his level (Figure 50) to gain superior hip position and starts a rethrow (Figures 51 and 52).

POINTS TO REMEMBER

- The tough part about changing level is maintaining good posture.
- Level is changed to set up, execute, finish, and counter moves.
- Strength and flexibility must be developed in the legs and hips to change level effectively.
- Changing level becomes more critical as the level of competition rises.

7

Penetration

To accomplish a takedown you must attack your opponent's upper body or legs. On all leg or hip attacks you must take a penetration step (or steps) to get inside your opponent's defenses and within range to complete the move.

The most important aspect of penetration is maintaining good posture throughout the advance. The hips must be forward and under the upper body to provide a good base of support to finish the takedown. This can be difficult because the level is usually lowered during penetration and you must guard against counters. Being able to maintain the correct position takes years of practice.

The two types of penetration used for the majority of leg attacks are the *center-step* and *outside-step*.

The center-step penetration is used for the double-leg (Figures 53–57), center-step single (Figures 58–61), and *fireman's carry* (Figures 62–65) takedowns. The photographs illustrate the similarity between the double-leg and center-step single attacks.

The outside-step penetration is used in the *high-crotch* (Figures

Figure 53

Figure 54

66–68) and *high single* (Figures 69–71) attacks. The high single takedown is also referred to as the *snatch*.

All of these takedowns are discussed further in Part III.

The beginner often makes the mistake of *overpenetrating*, or moving too far into his opponent. When this happens he sacrifices position and balance, and his takedown attempt can easily be countered.

If solid contact is not made during the penetration step, the takedown attempt should be abandoned. You should never stretch or extend yourself to reach an opponent who is too far away after penetration. You should simply return to your original stance by bringing up the trail leg to reestablish the base.

Figure 55

Figure 56

Figure 57

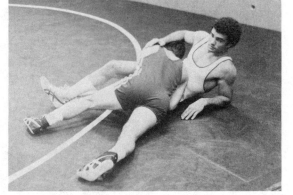

Figure 58

Figure 59

Figure 60

Figure 61

Figure 62

Figure 63

Figure 64

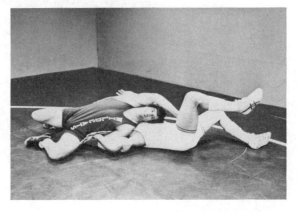

Figure 65

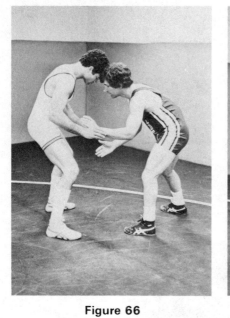

Figure 66

Figure 67

Figure 68

Figure 69

Figure 70

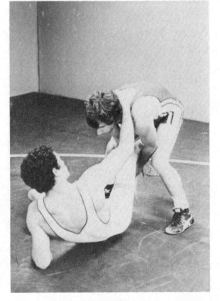

Figure 71

Penetration is made easier by setting up the opponent. This is usually done through motion and level changes. The best strategy is to force your opponent into a stationary position or one in which he is moving into the attack.

A good time to penetrate is when the opponent straightens up his stance. This makes it easy to lower the level and penetrate under his defenses. During a single-leg attack it is best to circle away from that leg so the opponent has to move it forward to adjust. As he does so, the leg becomes vulnerable.

During penetration care must be taken to keep your head up. When you are moving, the rest of your body tends to follow your head, so it is easier to keep your hips forward if your head is up. A heads-up position also allows for clear vision, enabling you to "read" your opponent's counters.

Also take care not to reach with your arms during penetration. To prevent your opponent from grabbing your arms, keep them close to your body until the last moment.

Dropping to your knees during penetration is another dangerous practice because it makes it difficult to maintain good alignment. On many takedowns, however, this practice is used. In these cases the knees should be in contact with the mat for only a split second. You can bounce or pivot on a knee, but don't use it as a base for any length of time.

POINTS TO REMEMBER

- Position is more important than depth of penetration.
- Keep your head up and your hips forward.
- Do not reach for the opponent.
- Do not overpenetrate.
- Keep your arms close to your body until the last instant.
- Bounce or pivot on the knees but do not stay in a kneeling position.

8

Lifting

Lifting may be the most neglected skill among wrestlers in the United States. Only in recent years have coaches recognized the advantage of lifting an opponent clear off the mat.

Lifting, which is essential in all wrestling styles, is used to finish takedowns, to set up pinning conbinations, to counter escapes, and to counter takedowns. In freestyle and Greco-Roman competition, extra points are awarded on some lifts.

The basic principle behind lifting is simple: once an opponent is in the air, he no longer has a base for support, balance, or power. Without that base it is almost impossible to counterattack.

Position is the key to lifting. To clear an opponent from the mat, leg and hip strength must be used. Lifting an opponent using upper body and back strength alone will leave you with frustration as well as a backache. By lowering your level and popping your hips underneath your opponent, however, you can easily send him flying through the air.

A lift can be set up in the same way as a penetration move—with a level change or a motion. If you catch an opponent moving

Figure 72

Figure 73

Figure 74

Figure 75   **Figure 76**

or coming up in his stance, you can use his momentum to help you lift him.

Care must be taken to protect your opponent or practice partner during a lift. Once you get him airborne, you are responsible for his safe return to the mat, at the risk of being penalized.

Figures 72–74 show the basic movements for a lift with an opponent. There are many different grips and holds from which you can lift an opponent, but the basic pattern of stepping in, lowering the level, popping the hips, and then extending is common to every lift. Beginners should repeat this pattern dozens of times before attempting to lift an opponent.

In Figure 75, B penetrates W with a double-leg takedown. The deep penetration allows B to pop his hips underneath W and lift him off the mat (Figure 76).

In Figure 77, W counters a double-leg attack by hipping in (powering his hips forward into B), arching his back, and spreading his legs wide. To counter this block, B slips his hands onto W's buttocks and clears him from the mat with a lift (Figure 78).

Figure 77

Figure 78

Figures 79–82 show a lift to finish a single-leg takedown. In Figure 79, W has straightened B up and forced the leg that was attacked to the mat. Note that in Figure 80, B's alignment is so good that after lifting W he is able to block with one knee, in effect tripping his opponent to the mat. Figures 81 and 82 show the finish of the lift.

Figure 79

Figure 80

Figure 81

Figure 82

Figure 83

Figure 84

Figure 85

Figure 86 **Figure 87**

A *reverse lift* off a center-step single is pictured in Figures 83–87. In this lift the head is to the outside of the opponent's body and the lifting arm comes through the crotch from the back to the front. In the final picture (Figure 87), B has driven W to the mat and has started to apply a pinning combination. Many lifts end in pins.

Putting an opponent on his back with a lift can be seen in Figures 88–92. This lift is called a *turk*. Figure 88 shows B penetrating for a double-leg attack. He lifts W's outside leg and drives forward into W in Figure 89. In Figures 90 and 91, B drives W to the mat, hooking W's support leg with his leg. In Figure 92, B has elevated the hooked leg and applied a pin hold.

An example of preventing an escape can be seen in Figures 93–95. W has stood up to escape, and B has followed him up and is ready to lift from behind. B lowers his level and pops his hips under W in Figure 94. In Figure 95 the *standup* attempt has been stopped and W is on his way back to the mat. A *rear lift* is an

Figure 88   Figure 89

Figure 90

Figure 91

Figure 92

Figure 93

Figure 94

Figure 95

Figure 96

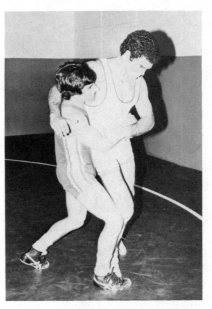
Figure 97

excellent way to counter the most common of all escapes, the standup.

Lifts are also used to counter takedowns. In Figure 96, W has attempted to throw a *headlock*. B counters in Figure 97 by lowering his level and lifting W off the mat.

POINTS TO REMEMBER

- Lift with your legs and hips, not with your back.
- Always lower your level before you pop your hips into your opponent.
- Lifts can be used to finish a takedown, to set up a pinning combination, to counter an escape, or to counter a takedown.
- Lifts can be set up by motion and by level changes.
- Remember to perfect the lifting pattern without a partner before you lift another person.

9

Back-step

Increased national interest in freestyle and Greco-Roman wrestling has put much more emphasis on upper body throws than ever before. This influence in turn has contributed greatly to the excitement of the sport.

Throws are fun for the wrestler and exciting for the spectators. Often the opponent is thrown directly onto his back for a fall or at least back points (points awarded for putting opponent on his back), in addition to the takedown. In international styles extra points are awarded for a throw with notable height, a quality called *amplitude*.

While it may appear that throws take great upper body strength, footwork and level changes are really more important. Strength has to be developed in the chest, arms, and shoulders and is used mostly in fighting for position. Once position is gained, however, it's the legs and hips that are critical.

Just as one takedown attempt sets up another, one attempt at a throw opens up opportunities for a different throw. The wrestler who can mix upper body attacks with leg attacks will be very successful.

Figure 98

Figure 99

Figure 100

Motion and level changes are good ways to set up throws. The rules of posture still apply to upper body wrestling, even though you stand more erect when you close with your opponent.

As in learning to lift, it is a good idea to learn the back-step without a partner first. Until you learn the necessary footwork and level changes, you will not have enough control to throw your opponent, and both of you could be injured. In Figure 98 the wrestler is in the basic stance. In Figure 99 he has stepped forward and into the opponent. Note the angle of the left foot. This angle will allow the pivot that will turn the wrestler's back into the opponent. The wrestler then lowers his level as he takes this step, his arms wrapping around the imaginary opponent. In Figure 100 the wrestler has continued to lower his level. He has taken the back-step with the following leg and continues to pivot. He has turned almost 180 degrees by this time and is ready to uncoil into the throw. Notice how close together his feet are. This allows for pivoting and maximum extension. Extension can be seen in Figures 101 and 102. The wrestler topples to the mat in Figure 103. If he had thrown a real opponent, he would be in a natural pinning position. After this action is perfected the wrestler is ready to attempt some of the basic throws off the back-step.

Figures 104–118 demonstrate three of the basic back-step throws: the *headlock,* the *hiplock,* and an *arm throw.* As you study each of these throws you should compare them with the basic back-step movement pattern shown in Figures 98–103.

HEADLOCK

In Figure 104 the wrestler has closed to a head tie-up with his opponent. In Figure 105 he has taken his penetration step. Notice how far across his opponent he has stepped. This will help him get his hips through. In Figure 106, B has taken the back-step and continued to pivot. Noteworthy are the foot and hip positions as well as B's lowered level. The extension and finish are pictured in the remaining Figures 107 and 108 and will be discussed in greater detail in the chapter on takedowns. The headlock usually ends up in a pinning combination as in Figure 109.

Figure 101

Figure 102

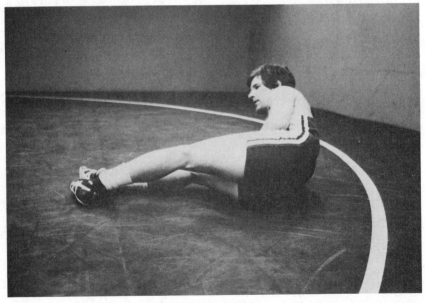

Figure 103

Figure 104

Figure 105

Figure 106

Figure 107

Figure 108

Figure 109

Figure 110   Figure 111

Figure 112

Figure 113

Figure 114

Figure 115

Figure 116

Figure 117

Figure 118

HIPLOCK

To attempt a hiplock B gains an over-and-under tie-up in Figure 110. He has also taken his first step. In Figure 111 he has not quite completed the back-step and has started his pivot. As the pivot continues in Figure 112, B has already started the extension. The throw is completed in Figure 113, with B going for the fall.

ARM THROW

The wrestler in Figure 114 is using an overarm tie-up to start his throw. The upper body lock is completely different from the headlock and the hiplock, but the leg and hip action is exactly the same in Figures 115–118.

Back-stepping takes hours and hours to perfect, but the wrestler who spends the time and effort will be rewarded with spectacular throws and quick falls.

POINTS TO REMEMBER

- Good footwork is more important than upper body strength.
- Set up the back-step with motion and with level changes.
- Lowering your level on the initial step is critical.
- The feet must be kept close together to aid in the pivot and to maximize the extension.
- Be ready to go for the fall. Your opponent will usually be on his back after the throw.

10

Back-arching

Back-arching takes courage and body control. It is difficult to learn, yet most wrestlers work at arching with great enthusiasm. The back-arch opens the way for perhaps the most exciting throws in wrestling. Throws off the back-arch are the "dunk" or the "home run" of wrestling.

Back-arching is allowed in freestyle wrestling but must be modified for folkstyle. In folkstyle the arch cannot be taken straight back, and the opponent must be turned to the mat to avoid a *slam* call. A slam penalty can be called against a wrestler in folkstyle any time he does not return his opponent safely to the mat once he has been lifted.

The key to the back-arch lies in the hips. You must not merely fall back and lift or you will end up flat on your back. Instead you tuck your hips under your opponent. The movement is so quick and powerful that, when done against an opponent, your head does not even touch the mat.

Motion and level changes are important in setting up the back-arch. To throw effectively with a back arch your opponent must

Figure 119

Figure 120

Figure 121

Figure 122

Figure 123

Figure 124

be pushing into you. When that happens the back-arch is accomplished simply by locking up and popping the hips under your opponent's pressure.

You should perfect the arch before attempting an actual throw. The basic arch pattern is illustrated in Figures 119–124. Figure 119 shows the starting position. In the first phase of the arch the feet are brought up underneath the opponent, the hips are lowered, and the upper body is locked in, as shown in Figure 120. Arching begins in Figure 121, with the hips thrust forward and up. In practice arches the head posts (Figure 122), and the wrestler turns out and on top of his imaginary opponent (Figures 123–124).

Figure 125

Young wrestlers often fear going backward when they do not have the control to keep their head from hitting the mat too hard. Figures 125 and 126 show a method of drilling with a partner to help control the arch until enough skill is developed to control the arch.

The *souplesse, bear hug,* or *belly-to-belly* throw is demonstrated in Figures 127–131. Figure 127 shows the wrestlers battling for upper body position. This is called *pommeling*. B steps in and body-locks in Figure 128. His following foot has started to come up underneath his opponent. In Figure 129, B has just begun to thrust his hips up and forward. W's momentum from the push has carried him over the top of B. In Figure 130 the arch is almost complete, and in Figure 131, B finishes by squaring into W for a pinning combination. The throw pictured is not as "clean" as some, because W has partially blocked the throw by posting his left arm on the mat.

Figures 132–134 picture a body-lock on the side. Notice the classic back-arch position throughout the throw. In international

Figure 126

style the throw pictured would earn extra points for amplitude.

The back-arch pattern, modified for use in folkstyle, is illustrated in Figures 135–138. The motion remains the same as the feet are moved underneath the imaginary opponent in Figure 135. The variance can be seen in Figure 136, however, as the wrestler twists instead of arching straight back. The wrestler finishes the arch by rotating further to the side, softening the impact by landing on his own shoulder. In Figure 138 the wrestler turns out to complete the throw.

POINTS TO REMEMBER

- The hips are the key to successful arching.
- Your opponent must push in if you are to arch successfully.
- Think of arching underneath your opponent instead of throwing back.
- Make sure you have perfected the arch before attempting a throw with a partner.

Figure 127   Figure 128

Figure 129

Figure 130

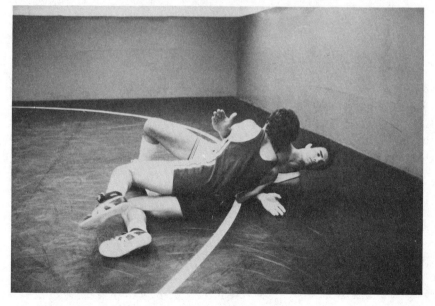

Figure 131

Figure 132

Figure 133

Figure 134

Figure 135

Figure 136

Figure 137

Figure 138

Part III: Moves and Holds

Basic moves and holds, as well as counters for them, are described in the following chapters. Chapter 11 deals with fundamental moves from the neutral position; Chapter 12 covers basic moves from the bottom position; Chapter 13 describes and illustrates moves and holds from the top position. These moves form a representative group; not all possible maneuvers are included in this book. Your coach will prefer that you learn these and other moves in a particular order.

11

Takedowns and Counters

Every wrestler must become skilled at takedowns. Because of new rules and current emphasis placed on wrestling on the feet, it is no longer possible to make up for takedown deficiencies in other areas.

The first takedown of the bout is especially significant. It puts the first points on the scoreboard, and it can set a pattern for the match by immediately putting your opponent behind and in a reactive position.

Each basic takedown in this chapter will be discussed in the following order: setup, penetration, and finishes. The counters to these takedowns will be discussed at the end of the chapter.

Reference should be made to the seven basic skills, especially penetration.

LEG ATTACKS

The leg attacks described here, including some variations, are illustrated in Figures 139–179.

Figure 139

Figure 140

Double-Leg Attack

This attack, in which you go for both legs of the opponent, is a great takedown against a good wrestler. If position is maintained, the finishes are clean and fast because the hips are controlled.

Setup

Faking a tie-up, changing levels, and circular motion are good setups for the double-leg attack. Get the opponent raising up in his stance to make quick penetration possible underneath his defense, as shown in Figures 139 and 140.

Figure 141

Penetration

Center-step penetration, shown in Figure 141, is used for the double-leg takedown. Since penetration is made straight into the opponent, care must be taken to keep the head up and the hips forward. It is important to drive up and through the opponent. If the knee touches the mat, it should be only for an instant.

Finishes

There are several common finishes for the double-leg action. The *post and drive* in Figures 142 and 143 is perhaps the most common. The *back-trip* in Figures 144 and 145 requires an extra step. The trail leg comes forward to trip the opponent. In Figures 146–148 a lift is used to finish the double-leg. The double-leg may also finish with an upper body lock or single-leg action.

Figure 142

Figure 143

Figure 144

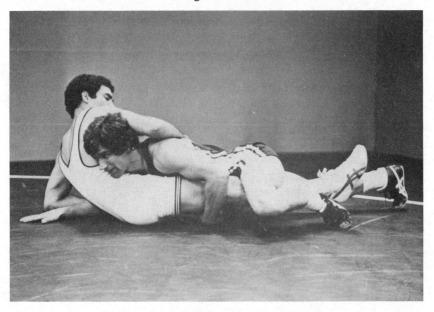

Figure 145

Figure 146

Figure 147

Figure 148

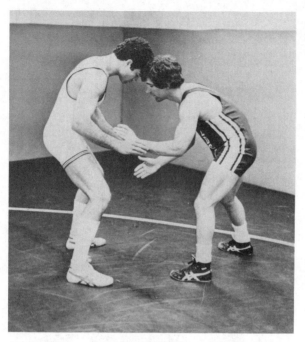

Figure 149

Center-Step Single-Leg Attack

Since just one leg is attacked here, the single-leg attack is easier to accomplish than the double-leg. The wrestler must be reminded to drive up and into the opponent to stay in good position. The head and upper body must not drop.

Setup

Circular motion away from the leg to be attacked is the best approach to the single-leg attack. Faking to the opposite leg and changing levels is also effective. In Figure 149, B has forced W to step forward with his right leg. Notice that B has moved his head to the side he wishes to attack. He has gained inside position with both hands and has moved the attack hand close to the leg he wants to attack.

Figure 150

Penetration

In Figure 150, B has used center-step penetration to attack W's leg. Notice that W's head is up and he is driving into B. B's right shoulder is on W's abdomen, not on his leg. The arm through the crotch controls W's hips. B's finish will be determined by W's reaction.

Finishes

If W hips in, B may go into a lift (Figures 151 and 152). If W is more balanced, B may change into a high single finish (153). Switching to a double-leg off the single center-step (Figure 154) is also popular. The wrestler should stay alert to the possibility of moving up into an upper body attack during his finish.

Figure 151

Figure 152

Figure 153

Figure 154

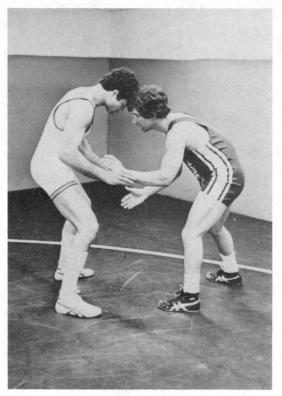

Figure 155

High Crotch Attack

The high crotch single is so named because the opponent's hips (rather than a leg) are controlled during the takedown. Many times, however, the high crotch is finished the same as other single-leg attacks. The big difference is that it requires more speed during penetration and a quicker finish.

Setup

This maneuver, shown in Figures 155 and 156, can be set up with motion away from the leg to be attacked. It is important to

Figure 156

be close to the opponent, and often an opponent's arm must be cleared from the point of attack. Head position again is important, and level should be lowered.

Penetration

Outside step penetration is used for the high crotch. This should be a very quick step. The follow-up and finish also must be completed quickly, because the penetration is not as deep as in the center-step penetration. Note B's head and hip position in Figure 156. He must maintain that posture and quickly finish the move.

Figure 157

Figure 158

Finishes

The high crotch can be finished in a high single-leg takedown (Figure 157). A lift (Figures 158 and 159) is often used to finish the high single. If the opponent steps back, the high crotch can be finished by taking another step into a double-leg (Figure 160).

Upper body finishes are also possible (see page 117).

Figure 159   **Figure 160**

High Single Attack (Snatch)

The high single, which features an attack on the opponent's leg at the knee, is one of the easiest and safest leg attacks. It is more difficult to finish, however, and is more easily countered than the others.

Setup

The high single is set up (Figure 161) by merely clearing the opponent's arm on the side of the attack. The head should be on the attacking side. Circular motion away from the leg to be snatched makes the opponent step into the attack.

Penetration

Outside step penetration is made by B in Figure 162. His lead foot is as close as possible to the target leg, his hips are forward,

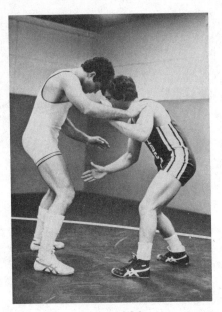

Figure 161

Figure 162

Figure 163

and his head is in contact with W. As B grabs his opponent's leg behind the knee and pulls up he must be careful to keep his elbows in toward his body. In Figure 163, B has driven into W and lifted his leg from the mat.

Finishes

The most common finish for the high single is the *dump* (Figure 164). In this move B quickly moves backward and lowers his level, snapping W backward to the mat. This is not an easy move, however, because W can counter by simply stepping forward. If this happens, B can drive into W in a double-leg attempt (Figures 165–167).

In Figure 168, W is stepping away from B to make the double finish difficult. This sets up the dump as B begins his circular motion (Figure 169), slides down the leg (Figure 170), lowers his level, and puts pressure on the leg to complete the move (Figure 171).

The high single can also be finished in a lift (Figures 172–175).

Figure 164

Figure 165

Figure 166

Figure 167

Figure 168

Figure 169

Figure 170

Figure 171

Figure 172

Figure 173

Figure 174

Figure 175

Figure 176

Fireman's Carry Attack

The fireman's carry can be used effectively with the high crotch series. It actually is a combination of upper body and leg attacks. There are many variations of this move, but only the basic carry is described here.

Setup

The best way to set up a fireman's carry is with circular motion off an *inside tie-up*. It is also effective to get the opponent moving into the tie-up with his upper body. The ideal tie-up for the carry is shown in Figure 176, with B circling away from W's right leg to set up the move. W has just stepped into B, and B is ready to penetrate. B's head is on the attacking side, and his attacking hand is close to the target leg.

Figure 177

Penetration

In Figure 177, B has taken center-step penetration. His hips are forward and his head is up, which is important to balance because both knees are on the mat. B's attack hand drives through the crotch and begins to lift W. The grip on W's right arm must be tight. B accomplishes this by squeezing with his fingers, keeping his elbow close to his ribs, and forcing his head into W's shoulder.

Finish

To finish the fireman's carry, B continues to lift with his attack hand and pull the opponent's arm down with his other hand (Figure 178). He then lifts with his legs and hips to pop W off his shoulders and onto the mat (Figure 179). To keep W on his back, B simply rolls over until he is perpendicular to his opponent.

A fireman's carry is often finished with high crotch action, especially if control of the arm is lost.

Figure 178

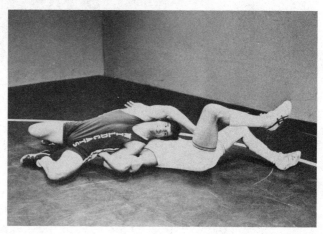

Figure 179

UPPER BODY ATTACKS

Upper body attacks are illustrated in Figures 180–207.

Headlock

The headlock is a favorite move of young wrestlers, and can quickly bring dramatic results. If careful attention isn't given to setting up the move and maintaining good position, however, the headlock can mean trouble for the offensive wrestler.

Figure 180   Figure 181

Setup

In order to initiate a throw, you must be sure your opponent is pushing into you. The best way to get an opponent to push in is to push into him and wait for him to push back. When he pushes back the throw is attempted. Remember, when you push in you are vulnerable to a throw. In upper body wrestling the wrestler who makes the move most quickly, with the greatest strength, and from the best position completes the throw. In Figures 180 and 181, the wrestlers are fighting for position to hit a throw.

Penetration

The penetration used for the headlock is the back-step, which was discussed earlier. Level must be lowered during the setup (Figure 182), and the hips must be rotated through (Figure 183). The wrestler in Figure 183 is in perfect position to begin his extension or finish.

Figure 182	**Figure 183**

Finishes

Finishing the headlock, or any other back-step, is usually done by extending the legs and pulling down or rotating the upper body (Figures 184 and 185). Once the opponent hits the mat it is possible to hold him on his back by keeping your hips off the mat and squeezing your opponent's head and one of his arms together (Figure 186).

Hiplock

The hiplock is a great offensive throw that can also be used to counter your opponent's attack.

Setup

The hiplock is either set up by an opponent's aggressiveness or from an over-and-under tie-up (Figure 187). The opponent must

Figure 184

Figure 185

Figure 186

Figure 187

be pushing in. The hiplock and headlock are set up in the same way.

Penetration

The back-step is executed just as in the headlock. B's hips in Figure 188 are not all the way through yet.

Finish

The extension of B's legs and the rotation of W's body down to the mat are also the same as in the headlock. When W hits the mat the pinning grip is slightly different, however. Your hips must be raised off the mat, and your opponent's head must be squeezed along with his arm (Figures 189 and 190).

Figure 188

Figure 189

Figure 190

| Figure 191 | Figure 192 |

Arm Throw

The arm throw is more effective in Greco-Roman and freestyle wrestling because it is difficult to hold a controlled position at the end of a throw. In folkstyle the defensive wrestler may spin out at the finish stage, and no points will be scored.

Setup and Penetration

Once the arm is locked, penetration is accomplished through the back-step as in the headlock and the hiplock (Figures 191 and 192).

Finish

Wrestler B extends and rotates to finish the arm throw in Figures 193–196. Notice that, when B hits the mat in Figure 195, he lacks the control he had with the headlock and hiplock. He

Figure 193

Figure 194

Figure 195

Figure 196

must quickly release his arm and bring it around W's head if he is to gain a pinning combination.

Body Lock

The body lock is a common upper body throw that can also be used as a counterthrow.

Setup

The body lock may be set up through an aggressive center-step into the opponent (Figure 197) or may occur after a secondary effort (Figure 198). Posture must be lowered, and the grip or hug should be applied as low as possible and as far to the side as possible (Figure 199).

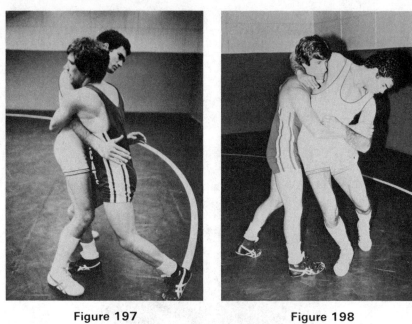

Figure 197   Figure 198

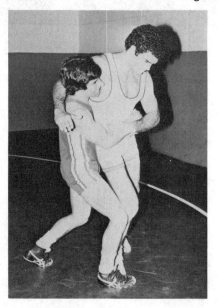

Figure 199

Figure 200

Figure 201

Penetration

The back-arch is employed to take the opponent to the mat in Figures 200 and 201. (Back-arching was described in detail earlier.)

Finish

In Figures 201 and 202 the opponent is arched to his back to finish the body lock. When W hits the mat, B must quickly move perpendicular to W to avoid being rolled.

Belly-to-Belly

The belly-to-belly is used most often in freestyle and Greco-Roman wrestling styles.

Setup

In Figure 203, B has aggressively penetrated on a center-step. W is fighting and pushing back for position and balance, setting up his throw. B's bear hug is tight, with W's elbows pinched in.

Figure 202   Figure 203

Figure 204

Figure 205

Figure 206

Penetration

B's hips penetrate underneath W with a back-arch in Figures 204 and 205. (Back-arching was described in detail earlier.) In Figure 206, B is looking for the mat, enhancing his arch.

Finish

In finishing the throw, B arches W to the mat and immediately turns to the pinning combination in Figures 206 and 207. From this position B must avoid being rolled through and works to a perpendicular angle with W.

Figure 207

COUNTERS TO LEG ATTACKS

The purpose of a counter is to take advantage of an opponent's attack in such a way that his penetration is blocked (usually with the hands), his position is destroyed, and he is forced to go on the defensive. In other words, a counter is an attempt to regain control of the match.

The three counters discussed are the *sprawl and crossface*, the *snapdown*, and the *lateral drop*. (In this section, the countering wrestler is wearing white.)

Sprawl and Crossface

In Figure 208, B has attempted a double-leg attack. W counters by pushing his hips forward and spreading his legs away from the attack. He also blocks B with his hands and starts to apply a crossface with his right arm.

In Figure 209, W has used circular motion to "turn the corner" on B. This, along with W's hip movement, has destroyed B's base. W is now on the offensive. He continues to apply pressure with

Figure 208

Figure 209

Figure 210

Figure 211

Figure 212

the crossface and reaches with his other hand to control B's hips. This is called a *butt drag*.

W spins behind B to gain control in Figure 210. (Notice that B and W are fighting for position to execute their next moves.)

Snapdown

The snapdown is so effective in turning an opponent's attack into points against him that many consider it one of the most important moves in wrestling. It is estimated that more points have been scored on the snapdown than any other takedown in national championship matches.

Figure 213

Figure 214

In Figure 211, B has started a center-step attack. W lowers his level and blocks the attack with his hands. W then moves his right hand to the top of B's neck (Figure 212) and uses his left hand to take control of B's right upper arm. In Figure 213, W snaps down B's head and arm, using circular motion. W then uses the butt drag as he spins behind B to gain control in Figure 214.

Lateral Drop

The lateral drop, also called the *pancake*, is a great counter-move because it puts your opponent on his back. In Figure 215, W begins the maneuver by blocking B's penetration with his

Figure 215

Figure 216

Figure 217

hands. W controls B's upper arm with his right hand and secures an underhook tie (reaching under the armpit to grab the top of the shoulder from behind) with his left hand. As W lifts the underhook (Figure 216), B tries to counter by taking a step with his left leg. W further lifts the underhook and pulls down B's left arm, driving into B and throwing him to the mat (Figure 217).

COUNTERS TO UPPER BODY ATTACKS

Countering upper body attacks requires advanced skills. Although the beginner is better off learning the basic throws before concerning himself with the counters, three types of counters will be discussed.

The first counter involves preventing the opponent from obtaining a lock secure enough to throw. This is illustrated in Figure 218 as both B and W struggle for position. Just as B obtains inside position with his left arm, W takes away the advantage by

Figure 218

pushing back inside with his right arm. This hand-and-arm fight-ing can be very intense and is called pommeling.

The second type of counter is accomplished by rethrowing the opponent or rolling through. This maneuver can be seen in Figures 198–201, shown earlier, as W attempts a headlock and B uses the body lock as a counter.

The third type of counter requires changing level or angle to enable the wrestler to complete his own throw. In other words, you must recognize your opponent's move and beat him to the punch. In Figure 187 (page 119) B is set up for a hiplock. W could counter, however, with a hiplock of his own by quickly moving his right arm into an underhook position and stepping back with his right foot.

12

Escapes, Reversals, and Counters

When starting from the referee's position, the bottom position is called the position of *disadvantage*. From this position a wrestler can score points on an escape (returning to a neutral position) or a reversal (moving on top of the opponent). It is almost impossible, however, to score points for a nearfall.

A big disadvantage of being in the bottom position is that you must carry the weight of your opponent. This is exhausting and demoralizing. In addition, when you are on the bottom you are in constant danger of being turned on your back for a fall or nearfall.

Because of these disadvantages, the bottom wrestler should try to escape or reverse his opponent as quickly as possible. The first move off the whistle is very important.

A wrestler coming out of the bottom position must be more aggressive than in any other situation. The first move might not result in an escape or a reversal, but it should at least put him in a position to extricate himself. The first move must be explosive and force the top wrestler to react in some way to create an opening for the escape or reversal.

135

To get out of the bottom position you must accomplish three things: fight for and establish good position, keep your back squared into your opponent, and control your opponent's hands. Adhering to these three rules is more important than using any individual move.

Good position is maintained by keeping the head up and the hips forward, under the shoulders. The head, shoulders, and hips should be aligned over the base of support provided by the feet and knees. If your opponent shoves you to the side or forward off your base when you are on the bottom, you should reestablish that base by pulling your hips and legs back under your body. You must fight for this position in order to retain a base from which you can launch an escape or a reversal attempt. Without the base you can easily be broken down to your belly or side, where you will be vulnerable to a pinning combination.

Keeping your back squared into your opponent keeps him from coming around the side to get a good angle of attack. Great wrestlers seem to have the knack of working bottom moves back into their opponents. It has been suggested that some of the bottom moves be renamed to describe more accurately the backward movements needed to complete the maneuvers. The *standup*, for example, would be called the standback, and the *sitout* called the sitback.

Establishing *hand control* from the bottom position requires great concentration and discipline. If your opponent's hands are not controlled, he can apply different moves and constantly tie you up. As a result, you waste good position, backward movement, and a lot of energy. If hand control is established, however, the top wrestler has difficulty maintaining control. Some coaches consider hand control the most important principle of bottom wrestling.

The three principles of bottom wrestling are illustrated in Figures 219 and 220. The former shows a wrestler who has partially completed a standup maneuver. The second shows the wrestler in a short sitout position.

The three bottom moves to be discussed in detail are the

Figure 219   **Figure 220**

standup, the short sitout, and the *roll*. Learning the specifics of these moves is not as important as mastering the three basic principles and applying them accordingly.

Standup

The standup is by far the most commonly used escape. This is probably because it provides the quickest way to establish good position. Using the standup as a first move can also set up other escapes and reversals.

In Figure 221, B is in a good stance and is ready to start his standup. His head is up, his arms are slightly bent, and his hips are curled tightly under his upper body. He is in as close to an erect position as rules permit in this starting situation.

To start the standup B pops his head and shoulders back and drives his hips forward (Figure 222). His inside foot (the one closest to his opponent) is moved just to the outside of his

Figure 221

Figure 222

shoulder. He also gains control of W's right hand and seals off W's left hand. In Figure 223, B brings up his other foot and squares his back into W. He also secures a *two-on-one grip* on W's right wrist.

To free himself from W's right arm, B steps away in Figure 224 and shoves W's hand behind his hips. It is important not to let go of this hand until a turn is made. In Figure 225, B turns and faces W to complete the escape.

Figure 223

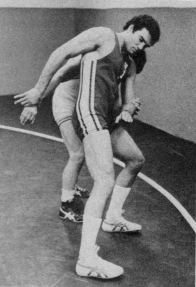

Figure 224

Figure 225

Figure 226

Figure 227

Figures 226–230 show the standup from a different angle. There is also a different finish, called the *cut-through*. The starting position in Figure 226 clearly illustrates the hip position. As the wrestler begins the maneuver in Figure 227, he establishes good position, squares his back, and secures hand control. To slip away from W's grip (Figures 228 and 229), B steps forward with his outside foot and cuts his arm through. He does this by stepping forward to allow for a drop in level. He also raises his left arm and slips his left shoulder below W's shoulder. By rotating his hips and lowering his level in Figure 229, he turns

Figure 228   **Figure 229**

Figure 230

into W. In Figure 230, B has completed the escape and is in a neutral position.

When a wrestler stands up he should retain a good stance with his knees bent. If he fully extends his legs, he can easily be taken back to the mat by his opponent.

Figure 231

Figure 232

Short Sitout

The short sitout represents a quick way to clear your legs and get your back squared into your opponent. Don't stay in the sitting position too long, however, but finish the move quickly to avoid your opponent's counters.

The starting position in Figure 231 is essentially the same as that used in the standup. Many times, however, wrestlers like to hide their feet (Figure 10, page 33).

In Figure 232, B takes a short step forward with his outside foot and begins to force his back into the opponent. At this point the hips are coming forward into the sitout position. The position

Figure 233

Figure 235

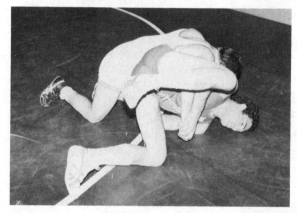

Figure 234

is reached in Figure 233 as B maintains good alignment, squares his back into W, and controls W's right hand. From this position B elevates W's hand and turns to his opposite shoulder in Figure 234 but doesn't expose his back. He must drive his outside knee to his own head, enabling him to recover to a strong base. He has turned to that base in Figure 235 and has turned in toward W to complete his sitout.

An alternate finish for the sitout is the *underarm spin*. As B reaches the short sitout position in Figure 236, W reaches over his arm in an attempt to counter. In Figure 237, W elevates B's left arm and lifts his hips off the mat. He starts to rotate his hips outward. That rotation, called a *hip heist*, is completed in Figure 238. W then continues to turn in to complete the escape.

Hip Switch

Another popular way to finish the short sitout is the *hip switch*. In Figure 239, B has reached the short sitout position. This time, instead of controlling W's hand, he cuts back with his right arm over the top of W's right arm to the mat. As he powers down with his arm in Figure 240 he increases his back pressure by lifting his hips off the mat. In Figure 241, B has turned on top of W for a reversal. When the top man feels the pressure of the hip switch, he often releases the bottom man for an escape rather than give up a reversal.

Cut Roll

The beginning wrestler usually enjoys learning rolls from the bottom. Proper position and follow-through must be maintained to avoid exposing the back to the mat. Rolls are fun not only because they produce a reversal instead of an escape but also because they usually put the opponent on his back.

The cut roll is a safe roll that can be used well in combination with a standup and sitout. Wrestler B moves from the starting position in Figure 242 by gaining immediate wrist control and pressuring back into W in Figure 243. Instead of attempting a short sitout or an outside standup, B tightens the wrist control by pulling the wrist down and pinching the elbow in. The wrestler has just started the rolling action in this photo by cutting the outside knee and leg under toward the inside knee (Figure 244). In Figure 245 the roll continues with B rotating his head and body under W. B has rolled under W in Figure 246 and established a position perpendicular to W. B then hip heists through to a belly-down position and pinning combination in Figure 247.

Figure 236

Figure 237

Figure 238

Figure 239

Figure 240

Figure 241

Figure 242

Figure 243

Figure 244

Figure 245

Figure 246

Figure 247

COUNTERS TO BOTTOM MOVES

Countering bottom moves is mostly a matter of being aggressive and maintaining good position. If the bottom man is fighting pinning combinations, it is difficult for him to establish a base and work his moves. If the bottom man quickly establishes good position, it is important to know the counters to his moves.

Counter for the Standup

The most basic counter for the standup for the beginning wrestler is the *follow and lift*. As B begins his standup in Figure 248, W is already starting to follow him. There will be intensive hand fighting at this stage because B is trying to control W's hands and W is trying to get a lock on B. As B comes to his feet (Figure 249) W has locked his arms around his body and has brought his hips under B's hips. In Figure 250, W steps to the outside to get a better lifting angle. This also blocks B's left leg. In Figure 251, W has lifted B and is driving him back to the mat.

Figure 248

Figure 249

Figure 250

Figure 251

Figure 252   **Figure 253**

Counters for the Short Sitout

The initial move from the top can also go a long way toward countering the short sitout. Once the bottom wrestler reaches the sitting position something must be done quickly to get him off his base or it will be difficult to prevent an escape. The two counters suggested are the *cover* and the *suckback*.

B has reached the short sitout position in Figure 252. W will use the cover to destroy B's position (Figure 253). W has moved up and over B and is pushing his weight down, forcing B's upper body to the mat. B has released W's hand in an attempt to regain his previous alignment. In order to get enough pressure on B to break him down, W must come high over the top of B with his body. His lower ribs should contact the back of B's neck. If this is not done, B will have enough back pressure to withstand W's weight.

It should also be noted that W is reaching for B's left leg in Figure 253. W completed the counter in Figure 254 by using

Figure 254

circular motion to spin on top of W. He lifts on W's leg with his left hand and pulls back on his shoulder with his right hand, snapping B back to the mat.

The suckback is used in Figures 255 and 256 to counter the short sitout. As B reaches the short sitout position in Figure 255, W hooks under his right arm with his right hand. W's left hand grasps B's chin. By rotating and pulling back, as in Figure 256, W drops B directly to his back.

Counter for the Roll

To counter a roll a *half-nelson* is often used. When the half-nelson is applied, however, it is important to sag the hips or the half-nelson will actually help the bottom man complete his roll. In Figure 257, B has started to roll. W has begun to apply a half-nelson with his left hand. B continues his roll in Figure 258, but W has dropped his hips farther and is driving the half-nelson deeper around B's neck. In Figure 259, W tightens the half and brings his hips farther toward B's head to flatten B on his back.

Figure 255

Figure 256

Figure 257

Figure 258

Figure 259

13

Breakdowns, Pinning Combinations, and Counters

Wrestling from the top position in the referee's position can be a lot of fun if you are aggressive. Trying merely to prevent your opponent from escaping or reversing will rob you of the joy of scoring points and going for the fall. If the top wrestler works for the fall, he is less likely to give up an escape or reversal.

Some feel that *riding*, the process of merely maintaining control on top, should be understood before an attempt is made to master pinning. The problem with that theory is that it puts young wrestlers in a reactive frame of mind rather than an aggressive frame of mind. The best way to ride is to apply pressure through pinning combinations, not simply by hanging on. If the bottom man is fighting a pinning combination, he'll have trouble thinking about escapes and reversals. The first move off the whistle from the referee's position is just as important for the wrestler on the top as it is for the wrestler on the bottom.

The top position is referred to as the position of *advantage*. It is an advantage for three reasons. The top man can start in good vertical position, while the bottom man is somewhat out of position because his hands are on the mat. After the whistle the top man can immediately make the bottom man carry his weight and thus wear him out. The position of advantage allows the top man the opportunity to be almost totally offensive.

There are two objectives for the top wrestler once the whistle blows. First, he should get his hips as close to the bottom man's hips as possible. Almost every escape move is designed to use the space between the bottom man's hips and his opponent's hips. The top man should minimize that space. Second, the top man should put as much weight forward, onto the bottom man's hands, as possible to keep the bottom man from gaining proper alignment and establishing hand control. From this position either the bottom wrestler can be broken down for a pinning combination or a pinning hold can be applied immediately.

BREAKDOWNS

There are several breakdowns that can be used to set up a pinning combination. In all breakdowns pictured in Figures 260–271 an attempt is being made to drive the weight forward into the bottom man's arms and to keep the hips as close together as possible.

Outside Ankle Breakdown

In Figure 260, B illustrates a good stance, with his hips close to his opponent's hips. In Figure 261, B drives his hips farther up into W and forces his weight onto W's arms. He also moves his right hand from W's waist to the *outside ankle* and lifts. B's left arm moves from the elbow to W's waist. From this position B is ready to apply a pinning combination (Figure 262).

Inside Ankle Breakdown

In Figure 263, B again drives his hips up, putting weight on W's hands. This time, however, the *inside ankle* is attacked with B's inside hand moving from the elbow (Figure 264). The hand around the waist remains and is used to drive the bottom man

Figure 260

Figure 261

Figure 262

Figure 263

Figure 264

Figure 265

forward. The inside ankle breakdown drives the opponent to the same position as the outside ankle breakdown (Figure 265).

Rotary Breakdown

The *rotary breakdown* not only drives the opponent forward, but it also puts him on his hip. From the starting position (Figure 266), B moves his left hand from the elbow to a position under his opponent's arm (Figure 267) and steps up with his outside foot. He drives off that foot and pushes W's arm forward. The arm on W's waist drops down and pries on W's right thigh. As B moves to the front of W, continuing to drive (Figure 268), a rotating pressure drops W to his hips and moves him forward. A pinning combination can be applied or the man can be broken down farther.

Spiral Breakdown

The *spiral breakdown* is similar to the rotary breakdown, but it involves more forward pressure. A half-nelson is used to help apply this pressure. In Figure 269, B is ready to drive forward. Off the whistle B posts (or controls) W's hips (Figure 270). This is very important to prevent W from turning in for an easy escape. At the same time B drives his left arm forward and under W's arms. B could also apply a half-nelson with his left arm. The breakdown is complete in Figure 271. W is broken down to his hip and vulnerable to pinning combinations. The spiral breakdown isn't easy to learn, but it is well worth the effort because of the pressure that it can put on the opponent.

Figure 266

Figure 267

Figure 268

Figure 269

Figure 270

Figure 271

PINNING COMBINATIONS

Pinning combinations are pictured in Figures 272–287.

Half-Nelson

The half-nelson is often the first pinning hold taught to a new wrestler. After B has broken W down to the mat (Figure 272) W attempts to push himself back to his base. This creates the opening for the half-nelson. B blocks W's far arm with his right hand, and his left arm drives under W's near arm and up into his head. In Figure 273, B continues to block W's far arm and drives with his leg to turn W to his back. To finish the half-nelson, B lifts W's head and controls the crotch (Figure 274).

If W tries to roll through, using B's momentum, B may elect to switch to a *reverse half-nelson*, shown in Figure 275. In attempting to gain the fall, B should remain locked in the crotch, stay up on his toes, and put as much weight on W as possible while lifting on W's head.

Figure 272

Figure 273

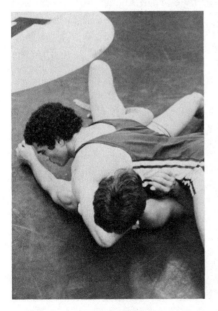

Figure 274

Figure 275

Far Side Cradle

Cradles are important to learn early in wrestling. They work well against good competition and can help turn a match around. Many times a superior wrestler who has been leading in a match has been put on his back or pinned through the use of a cradle. It takes a certain knack to recognize when a cradle can be used, but it is very important to master.

In the *far side cradle* the far leg is captured first. In Figure 276 wrestler B is attempting an outside ankle breakdown to set up the cradle. As he lifts the far ankle W attempts to counter with an outside standup (Figure 277). As W's knee moves toward his head, he becomes vulnerable to the cradle. It is important for B to apply pressure to W's upper back and far shoulder to keep him in a crunched position. This can be accomplished by moving higher and to the far side. Notice that B's left shoulder is directly over W's right shoulder. From this position B's left arm wraps around W's neck, B's right arm hooks behind W's right leg, and the hands are locked quickly. In Figure 278, B continues to move toward the opposite side of W's body and reverses his hips. He continues to squeeze his grip as he starts to set through. W is rocked straight back to the mat in Figure 279. Note that B is using his outside leg to elevate W's left leg to keep W on his back.

Figure 276

Figure 277

Figure 278

Figure 279

Near Side Cradle

The *near side cradle* is applied to the leg nearest the top man instead of the far leg. W attempts an inside standup in Figure 280. When he does so, B moves forward with his body, forces down on W's head with his left arm, and hooks W's standup leg with his right arm. B locks the cradle in Figure 281. His left shoulder is directly over W's left shoulder. In Figure 282, B drives W to his side using leg strength. The cradle is finished in Figure 283 as B balances on his head and toes to get maximum pressure.

Chicken Wing

In Figure 284, B has broken W down to the mat. He has established far side control by grasping W's right wrist with his right hand. He is also beginning to lift W's left arm with his left hand, while keeping W on the mat with forward pressure. In Figure 285, B has lifted W's left arm high enough to slip his own arm into the crook of W's elbow and across his back. This is the *chicken wing*. B is still driving W forward and has tightened his grip on W's right arm. In Figure 286, B continues to drive W forward by sitting through with his right leg. He then swings his left leg and hip around in front of W in Figure 287. This action rotates W to his back. Notice that B has not released the far wrist

Figure 280

Figure 281

Figure 282

Figure 283

Figure 284

Figure 285

Figure 286

Figure 287

and, by keeping his head up, makes it difficult for W to roll out of the combination.

There are countless pinning combinations and variations. The half-nelson, the cradle, and the chicken wing are basic. Once you have mastered them, you can move on to others, which your coach can teach you.

COUNTERS TO PIN HOLDS

These counters are shown in Figures 288–309. The most effective way to counter a pin is to avoid being broken down to the belly or side. If an aggressive escape or reversal attempt is made from the bottom position, it is difficult for the top man to secure a pinning hold. Even the best wrestler is occasionally broken down and may get trapped in a pin hold. Every wrestler needs to know how to counter the basic pinning combinations.

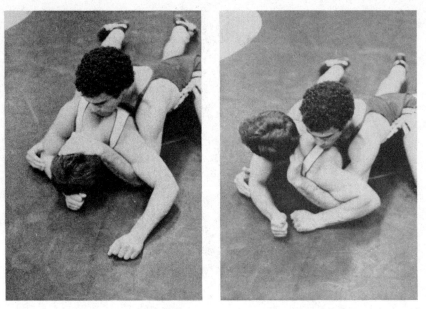

Figure 288   Figure 289

Counters to Half-Nelsons

Look-away

To break the half-nelson applied by B in Figure 288, W lifts his head and chest and then twists his head away from the pressure of the half-nelson (Figure 289). The *look-away* is a simple but effective way to slip out of a half-nelson.

Wing Roll

The *wing roll* counter is more spectacular than most, but it is also more difficult to execute. When B has applied the half-nelson (Figure 290), W counters by capturing B's left arm in the crook of the elbow (Figure 291). Notice that W has also used the look-away to break the pressure of the half-nelson. In Figure 292, W has started to roll B to his back. He must squeeze his elbow tightly into his own body during this stage of the roll. As B is rolled to his back in Figure 293, W steps over to gain a perpendicular position. This prevents B from continuing the momentum of the move and allows W to roll on through. In Figure 294, W has gained ideal position, putting B on his back.

Figure 290

Figure 291

Figure 292

Figure 293

Figure 294

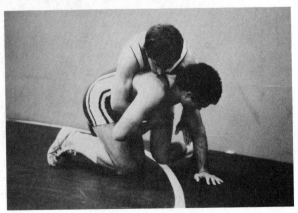

Figure 295

Figure 296

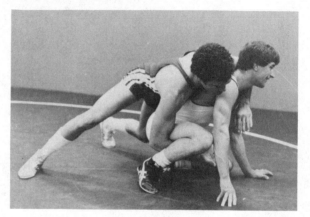

Counters for the Far Cradle

In Figure 295, B has clamped a cradle on W. To counter in Figure 296, W quickly reacts before B can adjust his position. W breaks B's grip through a powerful extension of his whole body. His head and back must come up hard while his trapped leg powers down. This must be done quickly before B tightens his grip by reversing his hips.

Since B has already reversed his hips in Figure 297, W must attempt another counter. This is called *elevating* the near leg. W has hooked his foot under B's near knee. As he elevates B's legs,

Figure 297

Figure 298

he scoots his hips away from B, arches his back, and turns in (Figure 298).

Counters for the Near Side Half-Nelson

The near side cradle is broken in Figures 299 and 300 in the same way the far side cradle was broken. This counter must be initiated quickly before B can drive W to the mat. The position for breaking the near side cradle is slightly different from that for the far side, but the same powerful extension is needed.

The *sit-through* is also used to counter the near cradle. In

Figure 299

Figure 300

Figure 301, B is starting to apply the cradle to W. In Figure 302, W immediately brings his head and inside arm up. He also elevates B's left leg with his inside foot. W's left arm must be freed to keep B from rolling him through. W completes the counter in Figure 303. This counter must be hit hard and requires confidence and aggression.

Chicken Wing Counter

The chicken wing is tough to counter because the top man has a great deal of control. The *limp arm* is used to counter the wing

Figure 301

Figure 302

Figure 303

Figure 304

Figure 305

Figure 306

in Figures 304–306. To free the arm W must crawl forward. This is difficult but necessary to create looseness in the hold. This forward motion can be seen in Figure 305. As W crawls forward in Figures 305 and 306, the trapped arm is brought forward in a swimming motion. This counter may have to be attempted several times before the arm finally comes free.

Another way to counter the chicken wing is to *post and roll* (Figures 307–309). In Figure 307, B has applied a chicken wing and is starting to drive it over. W has lifted his head and upper body and posted on his right elbow. He then uses B's momentum in Figure 308 to roll through. Note that W gains further elevation for his roll by posting on a straightened arm in Figure 308. He has completed the counter in Figure 309 by rolling the opponent to his back.

Figure 307

Figure 308

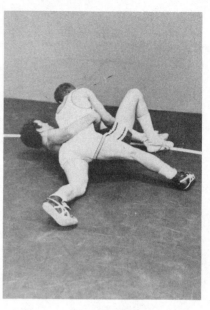

Figure 309

Appendix A: Weight Classes, Bout Length, and Scoring

WEIGHT CLASSES

U.S. Kids Division

Ages 9–10

50 pounds
55 pounds
60 pounds
65 pounds
70 pounds
75 pounds
80 pounds
85 pounds
90 pounds
95 pounds
100 pounds
105 pounds

Ages 9–10

110 pounds
120 pounds
130 pounds
heavyweight (over 130 pounds)

Ages 11–12

60 pounds
65 pounds
70 pounds
75 pounds
80 pounds
85 pounds
90 pounds
95 pounds
100 pounds
105 pounds
110 pounds
115 pounds
120 pounds
130 pounds
145 pounds
165 pounds
heavyweight (over 165 pounds)

Ages 13–14

70 pounds
75 pounds
80 pounds
85 pounds
90 pounds
95 pounds
100 pounds
105 pounds
110 pounds
115 pounds

Ages 13-14

120 pounds
125 pounds
130 pounds
135 pounds
145 pounds
155 pounds
165 pounds
175 pounds
heavyweight (over 175 pounds)

High School

98 pounds
105 pounds
112 pounds
119 pounds
126 pounds
132 pounds
138 pounds
145 pounds
155 pounds
167 pounds
185 pounds
heavyweight

College

118 pounds
126 pounds
134 pounds
142 pounds
150 pounds
158 pounds
167 pounds
177 pounds
190 pounds
heavyweight

Freestyle and Greco-Roman Seniors

105.5 pounds
114.5 pounds
125.5 pounds
136.5 pounds
149.5 pounds
163 pounds
180.5 pounds
198 pounds
220 pounds
over 220 pounds

LENGTH OF BOUTS

U.S. Kids Division

Ages 9–10: two periods of 90 seconds each, with 30 seconds' rest between periods

Ages 11–12: two periods of two minutes each, with 30 seconds' rest between periods

Ages 13–14: two periods of two minutes each, with 30 seconds' rest between periods

High School

Three periods of two minutes each

College

First period of three minutes, followed by two periods of two minutes each

Senior Freestyle and Greco-Roman

Two periods of three minutes each, with one minute's rest between periods

GENERAL SCORING

Takedown (gaining control and placing opponent on mat from neutral position): two points

Escape (breaking free while on bottom, gaining neutral position): two points

Reversal (defensive wrestler gaining control of opponent): two points

Nearfall (exposing opponent's shoulder to the mat): two points, three points for holding them five seconds or longer

DUAL MEET SCORING

Fall: six points
Forfeit: six points
Default: six points
Disqualification: six points
Decision by 12 points or more: five points
Decision by 8–11 points: four points
Decision by less than eight points: three points
Draw: two points

TOURNAMENT SCORING

Tournament scoring varies with the number of teams competing. Points are awarded for place winners, of course, and also for advancement in the tournament. Advancing by a pin can mean an extra point, as can winning by disqualification, default, or forfeit. Advancing in the championship bracket is usually worth a point. Winning by 12 or more points is worth ¾ point, in addition to the advancement point. A decision by 8–11 points means an additional ½ point. A bye, advancing without wrestling a match, is often given in tournaments that have an uneven number of competitors. If a wrestler wins his next match, he is given a point for the bye. If he loses, no points are awarded.

For further information about the U.S. Kids Division of the U.S. Wrestling Federation, write to U.S. Wrestling Federation, 405 West Hall of Fame Ave., Stillwater, OK 74074.

Appendix B: Glossary

Acute dehydration: the immediate reduction in weight due to fluid loss during exertion.

Advantage, position of: the top position in referee's starting position; the top position during a match.

Aggressiveness: a characteristic possessed by good wrestlers that enables them to be consistently on the attack.

Alignment: refers to the vertical relationship of the head, shoulders, hips, knees, and feet.

Amplitude: especially good height in a throw in the international styles, which is awarded four points as opposed to the usual two.

Angle: refers to directing an attack from the side as opposed to straight into an opponent.

Ankle ride: an attempt to control or break down an opponent on the bottom by grasping and lifting his ankle.

Arm throw: an upper body throw using the back-step in which the opponent's upper body is controlled only by locking an arm.

Back-arching: the seventh basic skill, used to throw the opponent to his back from the feet, seen predominantly in freestyle and Greco-Roman wrestling.

Back-stepping: the sixth basic skill, involving the specialized step and hip action necessary to begin the headlock, hiplock, and arm throw.

Back trip: a finish for the double-leg attack in which the wrestler brings his trail leg forward to trip the opponent straight back to the mat.

Balance: the physical attribute that allows a person to maintain good alignment both in a static position as well as during motion.

Base of support: the area represented by the weight-supporting parts of the body.

Bear hug: same as body lock, except a back-arch may not be used to complete the move.

Belly-to-belly throw: *see* souplesse.

Body lock: a move in which the wrestler locks his arms around an opponent's torso and attempts to throw him to the mat.

Breakdown: a move in which the wrestler flattens an opponent to the mat on his belly or side, usually when he is in the bottom position.

Butt drag: a finish for many leg attack counters, especially the sprawl; the hips are dragged forward while the wrestler attempts to spin on top of his opponent.

Calisthenics: exercise performed only against the resistance of gravity, usually repetitive in nature.

Center-step single: a single-leg attack using center-step penetration.

Changing level: the third basic skill; refers to the ability to raise and lower the body to attack and defend.

Chicken wing: a type of pinning combination in which the near side elbow of the opponent is hooked and barred across his back.

Chronic dehydration: the continuation of the dehydrated state for more than a few hours.

Closed position: a neutral position in which the wrestlers are close in a tie-up or a locked position.

Combinations: the variations in a series of holds designed to put the opponent on his back.

Conditioning: preparing the body physically for competition; involves exercise, nutrition, and rest.

Coordination: the ability of the mind and body to control and perform various tasks or skills.

Counter wrestling: a style of wrestling in which a wrestler allows the opponent to initiate the action and then attempts to score, taking advantage of the opponent's movement or momentum.

Cover: a basic counter to the sitout; the countering wrestler covers by driving his body up and over the opponent.

Crossface: a hold used to control the opponent's head by reaching across his jaw to the far shoulder.

Cut roll: a reversal accomplished by gaining wrist control and then rolling under the opponent, cutting under his center of gravity.

Cut-through: a method of finishing the standup; the wrestler raises his trapped arm and slips his shoulder from the opponent's grip by lowering his level.

Disadvantage, position of: the bottom position in referee's starting position; the bottom position during a match.

Distance running: an excellent method of conditioning for wrestling; should be performed for at least one half-hour per day.

Double-leg attack: a takedown attempt in which both of the opponent's legs are controlled.

Dual meet: a type of wrestling meet in which one team is matched against another team in predetermined weight classes; team score is determined by the individual matches. A wrestler competes only once.

Dump: a finish for the high single-leg attack in which the opponent is snapped to the mat by a squat or level change; often used in combination with the double-leg finish.

Elevation: a counter for a far side cradle in which the opponent's near leg is elevated in an attempt to roll him onto his back.

Endurance: the ability of the body to perform work over a long period of time.

Escape: moving from the bottom position to a neutral position.

Even stance: a neutral stance in which the feet are in a straight line.

Exercise: the aspect of conditioning that deals with a daily work load sufficient to prepare the athlete for competition— running, scrimmage, drill, weight training, calisthenics, jumping rope, etc.

Extension: a counter for a cradle in which the opponent's grip is broken through a strong extension of the back and leg.

Fall: pinning the opponent's shoulders to the mat, thus ending the bout (same as a pin).

Far side cradle: a pinning combination in which the opponent's far knee and head are clamped together.

Finish: usually refers to the final adjustment made by the offensive wrestler to complete a takedown.

Fireman's carry: a takedown that combines an upper body lock on an arm and a center-step leg attack through the crotch; the opponent is often thrown to his back.

Flexibility: refers to the range of joint motion allowed by the extensibility and elasticity of muscles and tendons.

Flow: the ability of a wrestler to move smoothly through a series of moves.

Folkstyle: style of wrestling indigenous to a certain country; also referred to as *collegiate style*.

Follow and lift: a common counter for the standup in which a wrestler follows an opponent to his feet and then lifts him from the mat.

Freestyle: a style of wrestling used in international competition, including the Olympic Games; also referred to as *international style*.

Greco-Roman wrestling: a style of wrestling used in international wrestling in which the use of feet or legs is limited; Greco-Roman style is also included in the Olympic Games.

Half-nelson: a common pinning combination; the forward arm is driven under the opponent's near arm and up over his neck or head to produce leverage for a turn.

Hand control: a necessary step in getting away from the bottom position; limits the top wrestler's ability to hang on.

Headlock: an upper body throw using a back-step.

High crotch: a takedown off an outside step in which the opponent's hip strength is neutralized long enough to complete the move.

High single: a takedown off an outside step in which the opponent's leg is attacked at the knee (same as snatch).

Hip heist: a method of changing hip position by sliding one leg under the other as opposed to merely rolling.

Hip lock: an upper body throw from an over-and-under tie-up in which the back-step is used to complete the move.

Hip switch: a finish for the short sitout in which the bottom man switches directions and cuts back over the opponent's arm that is controlling his waist.

Inside ankle: refers to the opponent's ankle on the near side in referee's position; a type of breakdown.

Inside tie-up: a move in which the wrestlers lock up in the closed position so that the wrestler's arms are inside those of his opponent.

Key: to note the opponent's reactions to a move and to adjust the attack according to that reaction.

Lateral drop: a takedown counter initiated from an underhook tie-up in which the opponent is thrown directly to his back.

Lead foot: the forward foot in a staggered stance.

Leg attacks: those takedown attempts that are directed toward the opponent's legs—double-leg, single-leg, high crotch, etc.

Lift: a takedown finish or counter in which the opponent is lifted off the mat.

Lifting: a method of finishing or countering a takedown attempt in which the opponent is cleared from the mat; one of the seven basic skills in wrestling.

Limp arm: a counter for the chicken wing in which the wrestler crawls forward and slips his arm from the opponent's grasp; also used on a standup and for a counter for an overhook not discussed in this book.

Look-away: a counter for the half-nelson in which the head is elevated and turned away to break the leverage of the combination.

Match control: the ability to remain offensive during a bout; to be active as much as possible as opposed to being reactive.

Mat savvy: the ability to concentrate during a match using all resources and circumstances to the maximum advantage.

Motion: one of the seven basic skills, which deals with proper position and balance when attempting various attacks and counters.

NCAA: National Collegiate Athletic Association; the national governing body for most collegiate competition in the United States.

Nearfall: a move through which the opponent's shoulders are exposed to the mat.

Near side cradle: a pinning combination in which the opponent's near side knee and head are clamped together.

Neutral position: the starting position in which both wrestlers are on their feet; a position in which neither wrestler has control.

Nutrition: the aspect of conditioning that deals with the intake of a balanced diet, including proteins, carbohydrates, and fats as well as adequate vitamins and minerals.

Open competition: usually refers to tournaments in which individual wrestlers are allowed to enter regardless of their affiliation with a team.

Optimal weight: the weight at which a wrestler is free from excess fat but still maintains a maximum energy level.

Outside ankle: refers to the opponent's ankle on the far side in referee's position; a type of breakdown.

Outside-step penetration: a penetration step in which a wrestler steps to the outside of the leg to be attacked.

Overpenetration: a penetration on a takedown attempt that takes the wrestler beyond his base of support.

Pace: refers to the frequency of various attacks as well as the physical pressure that is put on the opponent.

Pancake: *see* lateral drop.

Penetration: refers to the step or forward motion necessary to gain a takedown; the fourth basic skill.

Pin: a move through which a wrestler holds both of the opponent's shoulder blades to the mat for a prescribed period of time, thus ending the bout; also called a fall.

Pommeling: hand and arm fighting associated with gaining good upper body position.

Post and drive: a finish for the double-leg attack in which the wrestler steps out to the side with his trail leg and drives across the opponent to the mat.

Post and roll: a counter for a chicken wing or bar arm in which the opponent's momentum is used to roll him onto his back.

Posture: deals with the maintenance of good alignment and position in both stances and maneuvers; one of the seven basic skills.

Reading: observing the opponent in such a way as to anticipate his attacks or vulnerability; observing and reacting to the opponent's mistakes.

Rear lift: a lift executed from behind the opponent; often used to counter the standup or to finish a takedown.

Referee's position: the starting position in which one wrestler is up and the other down.

Rest: the aspect of conditioning that refers to appropriate sleep and recovery times before, during, and after competition.

Reverse half-nelson: refers to reversing the position of the arm around the opponent's neck in a pinning combination.

Reverse lift: a lift executed with the head to the outside with the lifting arm penetrating from back to front.

Riding: refers to controlling the opponent from the top position.

Roll: an attempt to gain a reversal by controlling an opponent's arm and rolling under him.

Rotary breakdown or ride: a breakdown involving the posting of the far hip and the forward pressuring of the near arm.

Scrimmage: refers to the practice of wrestling maneuvers in competitionlike circumstances.

Setups: movements, level changes, or fakes that cause the opponent to move into a position of vulnerability for a certain attack.

Seven basic skills: fundamental skill areas developed by the national coaching staff—posture, motion, changing level, penetration, lifting, back-stepping, and back-arching.

Single-leg attack: a takedown attempt in which the attack is directed toward only one of the opponent's legs.

Sitout: a method of getting out from the bottom position in which the feet are cleared to the front and the wrestler pushes back into a sitting position.

Sit-through: a counter for the near side cradle in which the combination is broken through a sitting action with an extension.

Situation wrestling: being able to recognize that given situations or positions in wrestling dictate certain responses.

Slam: a move through which an opponent is dropped or thrown to the mat in a dangerous manner; the offending wrestler is penalized.

Snapdown: a takedown, usually used as a counter, in which the opponent's head is directed into the mat as he attempts a leg attack.

Snatch: *see* high single.

Souplesse: an upper body throw using the back-arch.

Spiral breakdown or ride: a breakdown accomplished by posting the far hip and applying extreme forward pressure on the near shoulder (even with a half-nelson); involves a commitment of body position and weight to a "high" ride.

Sportsmanship: the quality of being able to compete with all one's might with a total commitment to fair play.

Sprawl and crossface: a counter for leg attacks in which the legs are thrown back away from the opponent and a crossface is applied across the jaw to the opposite shoulder to break down the opponent.

Sprinting: covering a certain distance at maximal speed; should be included in daily conditioning program for wrestling; usually executed in a gymnasium.

Stabilization: the process of maintaining a weight close to the desired competition's weight through careful control of diet and exercise.

Staggered stance: a neutral stance in which one foot is placed forward of the other.

Stance: the beginning position from which the wrestler initiates his moves.

Standup: the most popular way to escape in wrestling; the wrestler fights to his feet and then breaks away from his opponent.

Starting position: the neutral, bottom, or top position from which the referee signals wrestling to begin.

Strategy: a combination of various techniques, attitudes, timing, pace, psyching, and position to attempt to defeat an opponent.

Strength: the amount of power that is generated by the muscles of the body.

Suckback: a counter for the sitout in which the opponent's arm and chin are pulled back to the mat.

Takedown: a move through which an opponent is maneuvered or thrown to the mat from the neutral position and after which control is maintained.

Technique: the maneuvers used to score in wrestling; the holds, locks, throws, and counters that are used to control the opponent.

Throw: an attempt to gain a takedown and back points in one maneuver, usually using upper body control.

Tie-up: a type of lock or hold in which wrestlers in the neutral position struggle for an opening for a takedown—head tie, underhook, overhook, etc.

Tournament: a type of wrestling meet in which individual wrestlers compete for the championship of a specific weight class. Team score, if kept, is determined by the placing of individual team members in the various weight classes. There are many variations in the way tournaments can be conducted.

Trip: a takedown finish in which the opponent's leg or foot is blocked or kicked out from under him.

Two-on-one grip: a method of finishing the standup; the wrestler controls one wrist of the opponent with both hands.

Underarm spin: a finish for the sitout in which the bottom man gains control of his opponent's arm and hip heists out from under it; also a type of upper body throw not described in this book.

U.S. Kids Program: a branch of the U.S. Wrestling Federation that supervises, teaches, and provides competition for youngsters under high school age.

U.S. Wrestling Federation: the national governing body for amateur wrestling in the United States; provides promotion, supervision, competition, and guidance for the amateur wrestler.

Upper body moves: locks or throws that are initiated by gripping or stabilizing the opponent's head, arms, shoulders, or torso.

U.S. Wrestling Federation: the national governing body for amateur wrestling in the United States; provides promotion, supervision, competition, and guidance for the amateur wrestler.

Weight class: refers to the minimum and maximum that a wrestler must weigh to compete in a certain division. (*See* Appendix A.)

Weight training: the use of weights or heavy resistance to develop muscular strength.

Wing roll: a common roll from the bottom used many times as a counter for a half-nelson.

Wrestling: a sport in which two opponents attempt either to pin or to outscore each other through the use of various holds and throws.

Index